The Troll Tale
and other
Scary Stories

Collected and analyzed by
Birke Duncan & Jason Marc Harris

Duncan & Mossman Creative Arts, LLC
In association with:
Northwest Folklore
PO Box 253
Poulsbo, WA 98370

Added story:
"The Story of the Standard" originally published in Northwest Folklore Vol. 15, No. 1, 2004.

Added material:
Glossary

ISBN (XXXXXXXXXXXX)

Dedication

To Thomas DuBois, who assigned us to collect these stories.

Table of Contents

Preface to the Second Edition
by Birke Duncan.. 1

Introduction by Birke Duncan.. 5

Prologue: "The Story of the *Standard*"
by Norman W. Vance, Jr. with Garrett
Vance & Birke Duncan 7

Chapter 1 "The Troll Tale"
by Garrett W. Vance with Birke Duncan 23

Chapter 2 The Poltergeist Story
by Garrett Vance & Holly Luidl With
Birke Duncan... 63

Chapter 3   Experiences with the Fairies;
Tradition, Imagination, & the Media
by Jason Harris 92

   #1 "The Little People" Interview
   with Sean Gulager April 9, 1999
   Transcribed by Birke Duncan 98

   #2 "Fairies and Angels" Interview
   with Ashley Morris January 22,
   1999 Transcribed
   by Birke Duncan... 112

Chapter 4 "The River Boys"
by Bob McAllister
As told to an analyzed by Birke 152

Chapter 5 Four Anti-Memorats
by Gail Duncan, Jay Duncan, Garrett
Vance & Ralph Cheadle
As told to & analyzed by Birke Duncan 230

   "A Real-Live Leprechaun"
   by Gail Duncan and Jay Duncan 231

"The Halloween Prank"
by Garrett Vance 236

"The Earthquake in Japan"
by Garrett W. Vance....................................... 246

"Mr. Cheadle's Hallucinations"
by Ralph Cheadle 253

Chapter 6 Shadows of Tradition: The Role
of Belief and the Mechanics of Legend in
Tales of the Spirit World
by Jason Marc Harris...................................... 277

"The Haunted Mine"
Transcription Assisted & Edited
by Birke Duncan.. 283

"Ben & the Ouija Board"
by Ben Nguyen.. 290

"Tread Not on My Grave"
by Ben Nguyen.. 291

"Ghostly Inheritance"
by Ben Nguyen.. 296

"Ghosts from Down Under"
by Rachel... 297

"Grandpa's Visit"
by Chris Aynesworth.. 300

"Chris's Ouija Board"
by Chris Aynesworth.. 305

Place Legends, "Fairies of the
Field" & "The Ghost of Dunsany
Castle" by Samuel Barton 308

"Haunted Apartments"
by Gordon Dwyer.. 314

"The Haunted Hotel"
by Gordon Dwyer.. 316

"The Shadow That Should Not Be"
by Gordon Dwyer.. 318

"A Murdered Man's Revenant in a House" by Dan Parr............................ 319

"It Had My Heart Pumping at the Time" by Steve Clemens............................ 322

"Miscellaneous Hauntings and a Doppelganger." by Marta Montgomery and Kerie Frisinger.................. 329

Second Sight: Precognition, Fetches, & Wraiths "Visionary Family Reunions" by Gail Duncan 336

"A Fetch or Wraith & "A Murder Revealed in a Vision" by Leanna.................. 342

"A Life of Second Sight" by Denise.. 345

"The Demon in Saigon" by Ben Nguyen................................ 349

"Quite a Few Tales to Tell" by Billy Utsinger............................ 352

Around the Campfire– Our Ghostly Legend-telling Session Featuring J. Carraway Matthews, Kurt Batson, Ashley Morris, Birke Duncan, and Jason Harris............................... 361

Analysis–Motifs, and Analogues, Structure, & The Role of Belief.................... 366

Structural Analysis 392

The Role of Belief.. 397

Conclusion...................................... 403

Glossary... 408

Bibliography.. 412

About the Authors 430

Authors' Note to the Reader........................... 431

Preface
to the Second Edition

by Birke Duncan

The book has returned. Publication of *The Troll Tale & Other Scary Stories* in 2001 led to a long series of folklore presentations in classrooms, bookstores, libraries, museums, plus indoor and outdoor theaters in Washington State. The troupe of raconteurs usually consisted entirely of yours truly, but with frequent guest appearances by Jason Marc Harris, Garrett W. Vance, & Bob McAllister. We encouraged audience members to contribute their own uncanny experiences.

I also called in to a couple of talk radio shows, and once engaged in a 20 minute chat with Dave Beck on *The Beat* on KUOW.

These public appearances led to the book's inclusion as a required text in folklore classes at the University of Washington, Florida Institute of Technology, and Michigan State University. Those same

1

courses sometimes added our other text, *Laugh without Guilt: A Clean Joke Book.*

This new edition retains the original chapters, but adds a prologue. "The Story of the *Standard*" joined the repertoire three years after publication of the first edition. That was when I arranged an interview with an eyewitness to the event, Norman W. Vance, Jr.

Many changes have taken place since the book's debut.

Garrett W. Vance married a lovely lady named Montira Saisin. They moved to her native country, the Kingdom of Thailand. She works as a translator. Garrett thrives in a new career as a science fiction illustrator, short story author, and novelist.

Jason Harris, his wife, & two children live in College Station. He is a professor of literature at Texas A & M, and has had several stories and a novel published. My wife and I live on Bainbridge Island.

Bob McAllister frequently performed his one man show, "The River Boys," at theaters and bookstores. He co-authored a stage musical, *Joe Bean*, which was performed on Bainbridge Island, in Seattle, and as an off-off Broadway show in New York. He wrote two enjoyable books, *Even in the Wind, Even in the Dark* and *Thief of Hubcaps*. He also earned the title of Island Treasure, Bainbridge Island's version of knighthood.

It is with great sadness that I report his passing in 2014. Bob never retired from teaching, but simply moved his career to Olympic College. I watched his final triumph on stage when he stole the show as Colonel Pickering in *My Fair Lady*. He was proud of his marriage, his four daughters, and grandchildren. He came down with cancer, which he faced with dignity and courage.

One of his daughters, Heidi Jackson, called me with the sad news. She said that Bob was sitting in his front parlor, chatting with family. Someone said something amusing, Bob chuckled, and passed away. He died laughing.

Bob's story, and these other tales live on. Folklore has a timeless appeal, no matter when the narratives took place.

Birke Duncan, Bainbridge Island, Washington, March 2022.

Introduction

by Birke Duncan

This book is a special repackaged version of seven articles from four successive issues of *Northwest Folklore*, first published in 1997, 1999, 2000, and 2004.

We had originally planned to compile an anthology of memorats, firsthand accounts of supernatural experiences. The serialization turned our project into a serious academic study.

At no time did we set out to prove the existence of the supernatural. We intended for these stories to entertain readers. Nevertheless, the articles documented a great deal about continuities of folk tradition in late twentieth century American society. The challenge of writing for a scholarly journal produced a worthy educational tool for the study of folklore.

For that reason, we gratefully acknowledge the support and advice of Thomas A. DuBois, Ph.D., former editor of *Northwest Folklore*; and a grant from the

5

University of Washington Scandinavian Dept., chaired at that time by Terje Leiren.

Prologue:
"The Story of the *Standard*"

by Norman W. Vance, Jr.
with
Garrett Vance & Birke Duncan

This prologue will explore a neighborhood legend about an historic pioneer graveyard, and a haunted fishing vessel. We will see that the story and its subject were well documented in the press, and how the tale passed down to the next generation.

We start with some basic history of the area. Port Madison, on Bainbridge Island, Washington, was founded in 1854 as a lumber and mill town. After the mill's closure, the residents maintained a close-knit community.

The settlers' original burial site was Dead Man's Island, an islet between Bainbridge and the Kitsap Peninsula. Their selection, however, led to a macabre development. Tides eroded the graves, which were just four feet above sea level, and exposed the skeletons. Skulls of lost loved ones stared out at anyone sailing by.

Rowing and sailing were the principal means of transportation around Bainbridge Island, at that time, so the morbid experience became all too common.

In 1874, mill owner George Anson Meigs donated a parcel of his Port Madison property to Kane Masonic Lodge #8. Townsfolk moved the skeletons off of Dead Man's Island. They reinterred some on private property, and many others at the new Kane Cemetery, atop a clay bank bluff. The previous resting place later became known, euphemistically, as Treasure Island.

That story is eerie enough on its own. The Vance family, longtime neighborhood residents, have preserved the most mysterious tale to come out of the setting. I first heard "The Story of the *Standard*" from Garrett Vance, a gifted tradition bearer of ghost lore, in 1996. Eight years later, I interviewed his father, an eyewitness to the incident.

"The Story of the *Standard*"

Norman W. Vance, Jr., his wife Susan, and I sat outside under a tree in their yard on a sunny Friday the thirteenth of August 2004, at three o'clock. Mr. Vance was born in Port Madison in 1938. As an adult he, his wife, and two sons lived in different places around Washington, including the Columbia Gorge. They moved back to Port Madison, next to Mr. Vance's parents, in 1979.

I asked, "When did your father move out here?"

"He came out here in 1921. My uncle, Vic Hanson, owned a store in Port Madison. They had a pier out there, where Mosquito Fleet boats would come in. Vic used to sell stuff to people from all over Bainbridge Island. The only way out there was to go on boats. They'd sail into these little ports, and drop things off.

"My Dad also used to work for the Olsen family. Martin and his brother Pete owned property all over Port Madison in those days. They were fishermen by trade. The *Standard* was a purse-seiner. My Dad used to go fishing on it.

9

"The *Standard* was the oldest boat in the fleet, out in Anacortes. In his younger days, in the late 1920s and early 30s, he used to go fishing with Martin Olsen around Anacortes, up and down the Channel, out here, and all over the place. He was quite familiar with the boat.

"It finally got old and tired, and so did Martin. They didn't have wood preservative in those days. And so, the *Standard* started to rot and fall apart, as all boats do. The Olsens decided to scrap it, and beach it. Why they picked the sand spit, Point Monroe, I don't know. They had a lot of vacant beaches in those days. Nobody cared. It wasn't like now, when everyone owns everything.

"All the kids in the neighborhood used to play on it: Tommy and Anne; Ralph and Nancy Chatham; Betsy Hodges, who passed away when she was twelve; Rolly Bjornson; I don't know who else. We all lived around here. We used to like to swim off the sand spit, over there. We'd go running around on the deck."

The *Standard* had remained at the sand spit for over a decade, until one day in 1945.

"I'll tell you what I saw. It was one of those late October days. It was getting dusky outside, probably about a half hour before dark. It had been hung over with clouds all day. The clouds were gray.

"I came home from school. My Mom said hi and told me that Martin Olsen had passed away.

"I said, 'Oh, that's too bad. He was a nice old guy.'

"I walked through the house. I probably listened to a radio program (before TV days). A little while later, I looked out toward the water, which I was prone to do, and there came the *Standard* sailing by; not sideways, not backwards, but bow forward. Of course, she was pretty much of a hulk at the time. The water was right up to the deck line.

"All of a sudden, the phones rang all around the cove. Mrs. Ross and her sister lived up there. Mildred McLean called. In fact, in those days, there weren't so

11

many people living around here. Everybody was talking to one another. They all saw it. The boat sailed around the curve of the bay, and out to sea.

"Some of it was because of the high tide that day. There's a current that comes out of the lagoon. If anyone tampered with it, we would have seen it, too. Nobody went after the *Standard*.

"The morning of the funeral, we got up and looked out. The *Standard* had floated back and gone ashore right under the bank where Martin Olsen's grave had been dug. He was going to be buried that day.

"The next day or two, the men went over with rowboats and poles, and dragged the *Standard* back to the sand spit. It had never floated away before, and never again, after that. As the years went by, it rotted away.

"It was one of those strange things. I don't know what the odds are of that happening. It made the hair stand up on the back of my neck."

***

What follows next is an example of the tale passed down to the original storyteller's son. Garrett Vance is the principal raconteur in this book, supplying such vivid personal experience narratives as "The Troll Tale", "The Poltergeist Story", "The Earthquake in Japan", and "Norman's Halloween Prank." The latter refers to Garrett's brother, Norman D. Vance.

Before and between the times Garrett worked as a schoolteacher in Japan and Thailand, he used to host barbecues outdoors on his parents low bank waterfront property, facing north on Puget Sound. The gatherings culminated in scary story sessions after dark. "The Story of the *Standard*" began the activity, and Garrett then built up to "The Troll Tale."

Kane Cemetery and the Point Monroe sand spit are close to his parents' and grandparents' homes. The story gives the neighborhood a haunted history, and helps set the eerie mood for the rest of his repertoire.

13

Garrett's oral preservation of the story provided a valuable link to the past. His rendition is based mostly on his father's account, but also has input from his paternal grandfather, and neighbors who saw the events unfold. The following text constitutes the way Garrett tells the tale:

"This is the Story of the *Standard*.

"My grandfather moved to Bainbridge Island in the 1920s with twenty-five cents in his pocket, as he was so fond of telling us. He did odd jobs for a while, one of them was as a crew member of a fishing boat called the *Standard*. He could sign on during the summers, sail up to Alaska, and make extra money.

"The Captain and owner of the boat was an old Norwegian fellow. Martin Olsen owned waterfront [property] between Point Monroe, which is a sand spit, and the tip of Port Madison.

"My grandfather eventually bought property right next-door to him and they became neighbors.

14

"When my father was a small boy, the Olsens still lived here. They retired from the fishing business and were thinking of moving somewhere else to be closer to his kids who had moved away.

"The *Standard* was no longer functional. Mr. Olsen had taken it over to Point Monroe, which at that time was uninhabited, and he beached it above the high tide line. He'd stripped it, but the carcass was lying on the tip of the sand spit.

"When the tide went out, the local kids would go over and play on it. They'd stand in the wheelhouse, and run around on it; until the decks were caving in and it got kind of dangerous. The *Standard* was no longer seaworthy. It was a hulk.

"One day, I guess my father was seven years old, he noticed something strange. There, off to the east of the house, was the *Standard* in the water. It was floating upright. The *Standard* began to get underway, as if under

15

power. It shouldn't have been floating. Then it paused directly in front of Mr. Olsen's house.

"Phones rang all over the neighborhood because the *Standard* floated in front of Olsen's place. Later the thing started up again, silently moved in a circle all the way around the bay, in the front of all the houses, out to the tip of Port Madison. It turned with the curve of the beach and headed north: the course that it always took to go fishing in Alaska.

"Nobody could believe it. How could this happen?

"Well, it was that very afternoon when they found out that Martin Olsen had died in the morning.

"Do you think that was weird? Guess what. Right above the mouth of the sand spit is Kane Cemetery, a graveyard owned and operated by the Masons, of which I am a member. My father is a member. My grandfather was a member. We rule the world, by the way. I thought I'd get that in there.

"Anyway, that was the local cemetery where Martin Olsen was slated to be buried. The funeral was about five days later, I guess.

"Of course, no one had seen hide-nor-hair of the *Standard*. It was gone. Everyone thought it was weird. 'There went Martin on his last fishing trip' was the buzz around the island.

"Well, the morning of the funeral, my father and his parents looked across and there, directly below the banks of the cemetery, was the *Standard*. It wasn't lying on its side. It was beached as if it had driven up onto the sand, under power. It had been aimed there.

"He, his Mom and Dad, and everybody else went down to look at it. They couldn't believe it. Imagine a whole community dumbfounded.

"What are the odds of that? The *Standard* left at the moment Martin Olsen died, headed out into the open sea, and then came back. The odds of it finding its way back, just by natural currents, are impossible. It came back to deliver Martin Olsen's soul to his grave."

Historical & Folkloristic Analysis

This memorat (supernatural personal experience) is unique in the sense of its documentation. The Vance family had the foresight to save articles about the event and the vessel itself: a clipping from the August 18, 1933 issue of the *Anacortes Daily Mercury* and the November 23, 1945 edition of the *Bainbridge Review*. Neither item credits any writer. Mr. Vance ascribes the latter to the paper's editor, Walt Woodward. Further information comes from the *Review*'s obituary of Mr. Olsen.

Martin C. Olsen was born in Norway in 1882. His family immigrated to Seattle in 1887, and moved to Port Madison ten years later. He married Mayme Beaton "daughter of a pioneer family." Port Madison had been founded two years after the Seattle settlement. Mr. & Mrs. Olsen had a daughter Marian and adopted a son, Victor. The latter had a son named Harry.

The *Standard* was built in 1908 in Gig Harbor, Washington, and based in Anacortes. As of 1933, it was the oldest purse-seiner in Puget Sound and still employed its original engine. The boat required a seven man crew. It was 52 feet long.

Mr. Olsen died on October 26, 1945. His family funeral itself was held on November 2. The burial service took place later that day in Port Madison's Kane Cemetery.

The legend of the *Standard*'s voyage did not appear in print for another three weeks. "The Story of the 'Standard' Haunts Port Madison Folks Who Saw Events" cited no informant by name. Nevertheless, the article shows that the uncanny event was widely discussed at the time. It also asserted that the *Standard* stopped for a while in front of Martin Olsen's home. The article maintains that the vessel left the day before the funeral, but Mr. Vance said it departed several days prior to the service.

In terms of folkloristic issues, the voyage coincides with a motif that occurs in other narratives, when a ghost reenacts a scene from his own lifetime. That's according to Stith Thomspons's *Motif Index of Folk Literature*.

The tale is also a "simultaneous informatory experience." Finnish folklorist Leea Virtinanen's book *"That Must Have Been ESP!"* defines this scenario as one wherein someone "believes the […] scene witnessed occurred at the same time as the event itself (e.g., a clock stopping at precisely the moment that its owner died." The shockingly precise timing becomes a perceived supernatural link between two experiences.

The story at hand is far more dramatic than a stopped clock. Even if one doesn't believe in the supernatural, the vessel's departure and return in conjunction with Mr. Olsen's demise and burial add up to a stunning coincidence.

Conclusion

Part of this tale's longevity is geographical. The Vance family resided near the location of the events until 2004. They were in the process of moving to the Hood Canal area, at the time of our interview. The *Standard* represents an interesting continuity for them. Norman Vance, Sr. worked on it; Norman, Jr. played on it, and Garrett tells its story.

The Vances are a great help in folklore research. A total of four generations lived in one area for over eighty years. Bainbridge Island has lost a great deal in their departure.

Kane Cemetery is well maintained. Graves are all legible and clean, amid the green, manicured grass. Some moss grows around the edges of Martin Olsen's granite headstone. Garrett's late grandfather served as caretaker of the cemetery for many years. Norman Vance, Sr., and his wife are buried eleven graves away from Martin and Mayme Olsen. They're still neighbors.

A Sketch of the *Standard* in 1933, by Ethyel Holt

Chapter 1
"The Troll Tale"

by Garrett W. Vance with Birke Duncan

Biographical Information

This chapter will examine the principal supernatural experience of raconteur Garrett Vance, in terms of how it affects his beliefs and organization of his festive repertory. Familial storytelling sessions, like "The Story of the *Standard*" have honed his presentation style over the years. Garrett's performance skills also relate to his experiences as an amateur actor, English teacher, short story writer, and folklore fan. Sincerity strengthens his credibility.

Garrett Wayne Vance was born on September 17, 1965, in Auburn, Washington, and raised near the Columbia River. In 1979, as mentioned in the prologue, the Vance family moved next door to Garrett's paternal grandparents in a Bainbridge Island community called Port Madison. His grandfather had lived there since the 1920s. This put Garrett and his younger brother in the unusual position of being both newcomers and members of a well-established local family. The island itself is a thirty-five minute ferry ride to Seattle, and connected by bridge to the Kitsap Peninsula.

As a teenager, Garrett played as a defensive tackle on the Bainbridge High School football team. He later took an interest in school and community drama. Directors usually cast him as heavies, like Officer Brannigan in *Guys and Dolls*, a sailor in *HMS Pinafore*, Injun Joe in *Tom Sawyer*, Stromboli the mean puppeteer in *Pinocchio*, and Porthos in *The Three Musketeers*. He was elected high school Theater Club President in his senior year, 1982-1983. I mention this bygone activity because it relates to storytelling skills. Differences abound, but both endeavors require performance in front of a group, immersion in a story and, if successful, repeat performances.

Storytelling enhanced Garrett's career. In the 1980s, he learned Japanese, and taught English as a Foreign Language in Japan for several months. He returned to the Seattle area, saved his money, and moved back to Yokohama in September of 1991. The young man earned a decent living as a teacher in private schools, despite his lack of a degree or formal training. It speaks well of him that he could maintain long term teaching positions with no other credentials than ability and experience. He provided the following advice in a letter from September 7, 1992: "Just remember to let your students say something once in a while!! I tend to get carried away with amusing anecdotes." Apparently, Garrett adapted his storytelling skills as a linguistic teaching device.

While this gives insight into Garrett's gifts as a performer and group leader, a passage in a letter from September 6, 1992 ultimately led to this chapter of the book:

"I believe Scandinavia to be my spiritual homeland as well as genetic. I have a double dose of blood from the Vikings moving into Scotland, and those nutty Danish Frenchmen, the Normans, invading England. I'm sure I also have a good dose of Troll in me, which explains why

I can see U.F.O.'s. Did I ever tell you I met a troll in Sweden? If I haven't, tell me, and I'll set the strange tale down for you (though it's better live)."

He mentioned Scandinavia because I had decided to re-attend the International Summer School in Oslo, Norway. This also inspired the following request in a letter from March 24, 1993:

"I have a boon to ask. I would really like to have a small troll figurine! If you find one and send it to me, I'll happily defray all expenses. I could use the company, and it would guard against KAPPA, the froggish little people of Japan."

Whimsy aside, one notices how Garrett's folktale fascination crosses cultural boundaries. I bought a troll figurine in Norway and mailed it to his address in Yokohama. He paid me back in yen.

Garrett returned to Bainbridge Island in 1992. He had decided to pursue a B.A in English, so as to broaden his employment range. He enrolled in Olympic College in

Bremerton, and later transferred to the University of Washington.

Storytelling Contexts

Garrett visited me on November 18, 1993. We conversed for a while, and I eventually prevailed upon him to tell the troll tale. He was reluctant at first, because a living room on a sunny afternoon clashed with the necessary mood. The story's effectiveness relies on context.

He tells anecdotes during regular discourse, but saves supernatural tales for festive occasions. Typically, three to ten of his cousins or friends gather around a nighttime campfire at his parents' beachfront property, or while on hiking trips. Participants frequently request the troll tale, especially if they have heard it before.

Garrett has a well-organized festive repertory. He begins with "The Story of the *Standard*." He follows that up with his grandfather's narrative of a giant Sea Horse that surfaced just long enough to scare several fishermen. These stories reveal that reported encounters with the

27

unknown are traditional to the Vance family, and that Port Madison has a supernatural history. Garrett's repertoire also includes two first hand memorats: one deals with a roadside ghost in Japan; the other tells of a poltergeist in Germany. With the exception of the latter, the rest of his stories set the stage for the troll tale, the longest narrative of the lot.

The geography of the Vances' old property aids the atmosphere. Their lowbank waterfront yard faces north on Puget Sound, with a view of the bay, Mount Baker, and some of the Cascade Mountain Range. To the left are the clay cliffs, with fir trees and old houses. The neighbors have large yards and wide property lines. The Vance family had one hundred and eighty feet of waterfront.

Garrett adds: "To continue the scene, we have our beach in front of us and some old pilings going out into the water. Our boathouse is right near where I tell the story. Continuing on, we have a couple more neighbors, and then we have in the other end of the bay, another high, clay bank bluff; and this one has a graveyard on top of it. And then below the graveyard, there's a narrow channel going into a lagoon where we have a very long sand spit...shaped like a J. So that's the scene."

If a storytelling session took place, then it was the closing activity of a larger social event like a barbecue or family reunion. Garrett set it up: "I go down and make a beach fire out of driftwood that I've collected. We've usually barbecued and eaten already, so maybe we have some hot dogs and marshmallows for later. Everybody comes down, and we proceed to drink lots of beer. Everybody's talking, and having a good time; and that's when people get in the mood where they want to hear ghost stories. Sometimes I'll start it. Sometimes somebody else will, and it won't have to be me."

Rather than monopolize the session, Garrett traded off with other participants: "Like I'll tell one, someone else will tell one; and I'll tell one again."

His all-time favorite participants are Ingrid and Erica Selfors. Their father, Ed, and Garrett's father were close friends in high school. Ed Selfors inspired this text's follow-up, *Laugh without Guilt: A Clean Joke Book.*

Ingrid and Erica's festive repertory consists of a family tale, and previously recorded legends. The former concerns a Norwegian great-grandfather who resided in the mountainous area around Stavanger. He used to leave cream out for the invisible folk who would repay him by braiding the horses' manes. The farmer knew it was the *huldre*, or fairies, because no regular sized human fingers could create such tiny braids. His wife tried, but couldn't duplicate them.

"Other than that," Garrett explains, "the Selfors girls don't have any slam-bang tales of the bizarre. If they do, they're old chestnuts like 'The China Doll' and 'The Golden Arm.'"

These ghost stories complement the host's memorats because of the fright factor involved in successful fireside entertainment. Garrett occasionally performs these tales if he has exhausted his own collection. "Those were the only ones I had until weird things started to happen to me. It's like, 'I don't need "The Golden Arm" anymore because–heh–I have my own.'

"Telling ghost stories has always been fun, but I wouldn't have gotten into it so much if I hadn't actually had some of my own experiences. Those are the best tales."

Garrett saves the troll tale for later. He preferred to have a round section of vertically half-buried cedar logs as seats. "I can jump on it when I tell the troll part, and I'm all hunched up."

The session breaks up; participants either depart or sleep over at the Vance home.

This kind of private storytelling festival also appealed to Garrett while he lived in Asia. He and friends would have beach barbecues in Japan, after having gone skin diving, and Garrett told the tale in Japanese. His favorite context was at Mount Alishan in Taiwan in 1985. People in the area call their vista "the sea of clouds."

Some Chinese teenagers showed Garrett around and took him "to a round lake. It was very misty that day.

31

We were out on a jetty that jutted out into the middle of it. And in the middle there was a little, round pagoda we were all sitting in.

"And they told me the story of the ghost of the lake. Evidently some woman had drowned there and would rise up, and appear in the mist. We were all hoping she would appear.

"We were just swapping ghost stories and I told them the troll tale. They were freaked out. Two of them spoke really good English, so while I was telling it, they were translating it into Chinese for the people that didn't. So that was the most interesting telling of it, I think. One of the most fun anyway."

Garrett's inclusion of the lake legends reminds one of his multi-national folklore interest. It also aided the spooky atmosphere. The scene itself shows that Garrett can tell the troll tale to total strangers under the right circumstances.

During my first year of Graduate School at the University of Washington, I set up a storytelling session for this project. The same institution had accepted Garrett as an undergrad English major in 1994.

He came to my student housing apartment on January 23, 1996. Unlike a beach barbecue or a pagoda in the shadow of Alisha Mountain, we recorded the performance in my 10'x10' bedroom, which had brown carpeting, a desk, and window. An unzipped orange sleeping bag served as the bedspread for the long, narrow bed. My guest suggested posters for the bare, white walls.

I recorded two tales from Garrett's mental collection. The first dealt with horse-sized coyotes, who had chased a cousin's car through the desert in Navajo country. After a break, Garrett told his twenty minute troll tale. I enjoyed hearing it again and was pleased with the performance. Then we heard the tape. The coyote story turned out well, but every fifth word of the troll tale was unintelligibly high pitched. By the end, my informant sounded like a 33 ⅓ LP vinyl record played at 45, when he could be understood at all. We rescheduled the performance.

The cousin's giant coyote chase story probably inspired Garrett's novella and radio drama, "Riders of the Three-Toed Horse" a decade later.

"The Troll Tale"

On January 31, 1996, at 9:30 a.m. I met Garrett outside of Johnson Hall, the location of his botany class, and we walked over to my apartment. I set up a tape recorder, borrowed from the Scandinavian Department, but he took charge of it. I lounged on the bed, the machine lay on the desk, and Garrett sat with his back to the window. Sunlight from behind the curtain illuminated the right side of his face, while the left side remained shadowed.

The pronoun we, the beginning of the recording, refers to Garrett and his girlfriend at that time, Holly Luidl. The narrator later showed me, on a map, where the adventure took place. What follows is an edited transcription.

"It was the middle of September in 1984, and we were touring Europe by bicycle. We'd gone through

34

England and Holland and Denmark, and we went up to Stockholm, not really thinking about the fact that, at that higher latitude, it would be colder. We had a great time in Stockholm, then we decided to continue our biking and camping routine. This was the cheapest way to see Europe, in our idea. We set out heading west across Sweden, and our immediate destination was Karlstad on the top of Lake Vanern, or VAH-nern. I don't know how to say that any more, heh, heh, heh.

"I have to confess at this point, I was getting pretty sick of biking because it was raining almost every day. The miles were long, and up and down long hills. I was in pretty good shape, but it wasn't my thing. Biking was Holly's thing. I wasn't thrilled about leaving the comforts of the city to be actually out doing this again.

"But the countryside was beautiful [pause] through the rain and the mist.

"We had a map and were looking for the little triangles that meant campground. And we found one that was about–I don't know–ten miles or so south of a town that was on our route. It would be just a brief, southerly detour."

The town, by the way, was Nykvarn, 59 degrees, 10 minutes north; 17 degrees, 27 minutes east.

"So, we biked and biked and biked, and we left the town; and it just seemed a lot farther than ten miles, somehow. We were up and down these hills, and we were out in farmland, and entered the forest.

"I was pretty much actively praying that my bicycle would break down. I think that subconsciously I was guiding it into the biggest potholes alongside the road, and basically beating the crap out of it; hoping it would break down, and that we could buy Eurail passes, and that we could have a nice fun time.

"So, it happened that on that day, it really did. I totally destroyed the derailleur on a big rock. I was saying, 'Oh, oh, no. How badly is it broken?'

"Holly's like, 'Oh, it's terrible. It's totaled. This is a Japanese bike. I can't get parts.'

"I'm like, 'Oh, no.' Heh, heh, heh! 'How awful.'

36

"But as far as the day went, we were kind of screwed because it meant I had to push my bike for another additional seven miles. So, we commenced pushing. Holly would ride a mile ahead and take a look to see if we were there yet, and I would slog along and coast down hills when I could, and push the bike up them.

"It seems like the countryside evened out and we were in the middle of nowhere. There were no houses anymore, when we found the cut-off road to the campground. It was a dirt road. It had been raining all day, but at this point, it had cleared up. It actually got kind of nice out, which was comforting. It was good. I dried out a little bit.

"We pushed our bikes down this long, twisty, windy dirt road, and came out to a parking lot. Holly was awfully upset to find out that the campground was closed for the season, which didn't surprise me any, but she had had this big fantasy about taking a hot shower. She was almost in tears when she rattled the door. I tried to pick the lock, but it didn't work [chuckle], not that there would have been any hot water anyway.

"I tried to be the morale booster and say, 'Well, it doesn't matter, you know. Let's have a good dinner. This is a beautiful place.'

"And it was. It was a big lake, probably a mile across. There were no houses anywhere on shore. It was a crescent-shaped inlet that the campground was on. And to the west was a big hill with fir trees on it, or pines, or whatever. Conifers. And then to the south there was a peninsula going out with a few birch trees clinging to the rocks, and then some big boulders out into the water. So it was very scenic. It was really pretty."

For the record, this was Lake Yngern.

"Holly set up the tent while I got dinner going, because at this point it was about four o'clock in the afternoon. It had taken us a long time to push my bike there. As I was cooking, I had a tingly feeling that I was being watched. And I would do things like: I'd turn around real quick, and no one would be there."

Garrett jerked his upper body and stared briefly toward the closet door, then turned back to the tape recorder.

"Or, I'd think, 'Holly's looking at me.' I'd turn around and she'd be off doing whatever.

"I started to get a little nervous, but I just thought, 'Nah, it can't be. It's just my imagination, or it's squirrels, or something, right?'

"I didn't tell Holly about my feeling because she would have laughed at me. Heh, heh, heh, heh, heh! She would have made fun of me.

"We were just sitting down in the middle of dinner when I looked up and saw this huge, black wall of clouds moving towards us from the north, through the trees. It was just [pause] deadly looking. I could hear the thunder off in the distance, rumbling away. I said, "We gotta get in the tent now.'

"We hurriedly finished dinner. And we hadn't even like washed the dishes or anything when the rain started to come down. So, pretty basically, we just dove into the tent.

"We didn't get back out because it was a storm. The temperature must have dropped twenty degrees, I swear. Well, maybe not that much, but it got damn–it got darn cold. We put on about three changes of clothes because even our sleeping bags weren't really warm enough at this point. And they were damp anyway. Some rain had gotten into them on the day's journey.

"There we were in our tent. Fortunately, we put the tent between three very large trees. I think they were maples. And it was kind of protected from the worst of the wind. So, we had our sleeping bags zipped together, and we were both curled up in kind of a fetal position with our backs to each other.

"That was about five o'clock at night–I mean in the evening–but it was pitch black. As soon as the storm came, it got dark. The wind was howling, and I couldn't sleep. I tried to sleep, but I couldn't. I laid there for hours, just listening to the wind, and kind of nodding off and then waking up again, and listening to the wind some more.

"Holly was snoring. She was asleep. She probably wouldn't like it that I told you she was snoring, but don't tell her. Heh, heh, heh, heh! You're gonna hear more things about Holly she wouldn't want anyone to know.

"I started to hear voices in the wind. And of course at first I thought, 'It's just my imagination. It's just the sound of the wind through the trees.'

"And they came closer. I realized, 'You know, those are voices. I'm really hearing someone talking.'

"The tone that they had was kind of guttural. It was like 'Rurrararrararrr' this growly kind of stuff. And I could understand enough Swedish just from going to Port Madison Lutheran [Church] all those years, to know that it wasn't normal Swedish. It sounded really gruff and crude. There was something about it. It freaked me out.

"I thought, 'Who the hell is out in the middle of nowhere in this storm, running around in the woods?'

There weren't any houses nearby that I could see. I mean, all there was, was the main building with showers and stuff; the office, and a couple of summer houses. I mean just like one-room cabins. And they were all abandoned. No cars. Nothing in the parking lot.

I thought, 'This is kind of weird, but hopefully they won't notice us.'

"Well, it was just at that moment when Holly woke up and said [moan], 'I gotta go to the bathroom.'

"Heh, he, heh! I thought, 'NO!'

"So I said, "Well, maybe you should wait until morning.'

"She said [nasal whine]: 'I can't!'

"And I said, 'Well, it's really cold out there.'

"At this point, the rain had stopped but the wind was blowing pretty hard. I said, 'It's really cold out there. I mean, I, I, I, I think it's dangerous.'

"She's like, 'What? Are you kidding? Come on. I grew up hiking in the Olympics [Olympic Mountains], you know? Big deal.'

"And I'm thinking, 'Oh, well.'

"I didn't want to tell her that I was hearing voices out in the woods, because it might alarm her. Why?! Definitely, Holly was a lot braver person than me. Heh, heh, heh. She wouldn't have been scared of this. But for some reason, I was being protective and didn't want to alarm her; which was stupid.

"I said, 'If you've really got to go, then do it near the tent. I don't care what you have to do. Just do it near the tent, and don't stray far away.'

"And she's like, 'Yeah, yeah, yeah, right, right.'

"She unzips the tent and gets out. And while she's going to the bathroom, I'm talking to her: 'Hey, how, how's everything going?'

"She's like, 'Shut up! Leave me alone!' [snicker]

"She doesn't understand why I want to keep in contact with her. I'm listening at the same time to see, 'Well, do I hear the voices? I don't hear them anymore. Well, great. Now they've heard us talking, and they're watching her in the bushes, or maybe we scared them off.'

"I'm waiting for her to come back in. And I'm just lying on my side.

"How brave of me to get up and stand guard while she goes to the bathroom. But you see, there was danger. She probably would have gotten mad at me.

"No, she definitely would have gotten mad at me if I'd tried that. So that's my rationale. I stayed in the tent talking to her.

"She got back in, and as she was getting into the tent, she had left the door open. All of a sudden on my arm, I get pinched really hard. Like, imagine someone taking their strongest fingers and going RRR! Right here."

Garrett demonstrated with his left index finger and thumb on his right bicep.

"And it hurt. It really hurt a lot. I just yelled, 'Weah! What the hell did you do that for?'

"And Holly says, 'What?'

"I said, 'Y-you pinched me.'

"'I did not.'

44

"'You did, too. You pinched me when you were getting back into the tent.'

"She said, 'What the hell are you talking about?'

"I'm lying on my side, with my eyes closed. Well, it was dark. I'm like, 'That hurt.' I'm rubbing my arm [whimper]: 'That really hurt.'

"She said, 'Listen, I don't know what you're talking about.'

"I said, 'You pinched me.'

'I did not'

"I said, 'I was only trying to help [whimper] wuh, wuh, wuh!'

"'You're, you're out of your mind.'

"For some reason, I really wanted her to confess. I wanted her to say, 'Yes, I pinched you.' So I'm like: 'You pinched me.'

"'Did not.'

"'Did too.'

"'Did not.'

"Did too.

"Did not.'

"Did too.'

"Finally, she says, "Listen. If you don't shut up, I'm gonna kill you.'

"And I believed her, so I shut up.

"I started to think, 'Okay, okay. I've got to think this through. Holly didn't pinch me. I didn't pinch me. Who pinched me?'

"It was at that moment that I rolled over onto my back and I just had this feeling. Every hair on my body stood up, and I'm very hairy. My entire body raised the sleeping bag an inch.

"Holly is curled up in a fetal position on my right, with her back to me; now angry at me. Heh, heh!

"I lift my head. There at the back of the tent is a figure. And I can see because there's an old mercury vapor parking lamp, like an old street light in the parking lot, that's shining through the trees.

"What I'm seeing is a silhouette of something that's the size of an eleven-year-old kid. It was human shaped, and it was sitting on its haunches, with its elbows on its knees, with its legs splayed."

Garrett, seated in the black swivel chair, imitated the intruder's position.

"I could see that it was hairy. It was furry. I could see filaments of hair through the street light; through the glow. The most alarming thing about it was that it had pointy ears. It had big, fox-like ears sticking out of the side of its head; like giant Spock ears. And they were hairy, too. It was looking at me. I couldn't see its face, but I knew: 'I'm looking at it; it's looking at me.'

"As it was sitting there, it would slowly shift its weight from one leg to the other."

Garrett leaned his right forearm on his right thigh, then leaned his left forearm on his left thigh. He repeated the motion twice.

"I couldn't see if it had a tail or not. I don't know that. But there it was. And I'm like: 'Oh, oh, oh! My God! Nguh, nguh, nguh!'

"I was completely stunned. I was immobilized with fear as I'm staring at this thing. It's what pinched me. I don't know how long I lay there, staring at this thing. It seemed like an hour, but it was probably only five minutes. Neither of us moved, so I thought, 'Well, okay.'

"Finally, I started to come clear a little bit. I thought, 'Okay, I gotta do something. I gotta get this thing out of here.'

"I started to think, 'I need a weapon. What can I do? What can I do?'

"I realized that I'd left my Swiss Army knife out with all of the cooking stuff, when we'd run in from the rain. I started to think [stage whisper]: 'Okay, okay: Plan B.'

"I came up with a great plan. I would conquer this thing with modern science. Because I knew that on the left, in the corner of the tent, was where I always kept my waterproof flashlight with the krypton bulb. And that's a pretty hefty flashlight. My whole plan was that I was gonna count to three, grab the flashlight, turn it on, blind it, and then beat the crap out of it with the flashlight.

"I'm like: 'Okay. [panting] And it's just shifting its weight, shifting its weight, watching me, watching me...

"Holly doesn't see. She's not asleep, but she hasn't noticed it.

"I'm thinking, 'Okay, here we go. Count to three. I'm gonna go. One. [nervous laughter] Heh heh. Twooooo [pause] Two-and-a-half. I don't want to do this, but I know that I must. So finally: 'Three!'

"I reach over. My hand lands on the flashlight, so I'm kind of twisted. At that very moment: FOOOSH!"

Garrett loomed up with his hands overlapped and arms raised over his head in a diver's position. Then he resumed his seat.

"The thing launches itself right at me. I feel its fur brushing my back, and the back of my arm, and my shoulder.

"Holly evidently feels it, too, because she screams: 'AAAAAAH!'

"Then I screamed, 'AAAAAAAAAAH!'

"I'm trying to get the flashlight. The thing–hoosh–
is gone. It just passed us, and went out the door. The tent
flap is flapping back and forth like one of those swinging
doors in old saloons. You know how they are. I got the
flashlight on, and turned over on my stomach. I was
shining it out the tent flap, and there's nothing. There are
no footprints. There's nothing but raindrops in my
flashlight beam.

"Holly's like: 'What the hell was that? What the
hell was that? Something furry. Something furry touched
me. Aaah!'

"I'm like: 'I don't know. It was in the tent. Aaah!
B-b-b-b-b-b!'

"I'm freaking out. At this point, I get up and get
out and start doing [acapella scatting of an action tune]:
'Duh-duh-duh. [Normal voice again] You can't see me on
the tape recorder, but I'm shining the light all over the
place, in a defensive posture.

"I was mumbling: 'Well, here we are. If you want to come back and kill us, be my guest. I'm going back to sleep.'

"I got back in the tent and she said, 'What was it? What was it?'

"I said, 'Look, I, I think it was a troll.'

"'What?'

"'Holly, it was small, it was furry, it was man-like, it had pointy ears. It was a troll. What else could it be?'

"'Maybe it was an escaped monkey from the zoo.'

"'Oh, yeah, it's gonna survive in this weather, in northern Europe.'

"She says, 'What are we gonna do?'

"I said, 'Nothing. I'm gonna go back to bed. You can stand guard. If it comes back and kills us, there's nothing we can do about it.'

"We zipped up the tent and went back to sleep. As I was drifting off to sleep, I started to think to myself, 'You know, if Holly had remembered to close the tent flap, then that thing wouldn't have been able to get out.'

"I just imagined it bouncing around inside, with me trying to get the flashlight on. It would have been really bad. Fortunately, she didn't. We got into the argument right away, so she forgot. And so the tent flap was open, which was a good thing. [sigh] Oh!

"The next morning, we got up. And I searched the camp and found some of our bread had been stolen. That was the only thing that they–or it–took. I never heard any other voices the night before, after that. The voices were gone, so I have to assume there was a connection there.

"I started to think, 'What was it that happened last night?' I had this feeling that whatever it was didn't mean to harm us, but it certainly did mean to scare us. It was a trickster. It was a mischievous creature. Here were these two dumb Americans out in the woods, in the middle of the night. What a perfect opportunity.

"How many folktales are there where something exactly like that happens? There's lots: in England, in Germany, in Scandinavia. There's lots of stories like this of the little people hassling the wayfarers.

"We were having breakfast at a picnic table when some kids rode up on bicycles. They were from the local town, and they were coming to go fishing. At first, they asked us if we were Finnish. Heh, heh, heh! That would explain why we were camping in the middle of September.

"'No, we're Americans.'

"Oh, well, I guess that explains it too.'

"Only crazy people, I guess. Finns and Americans are the only ones who would be dumb enough to go camping at this time of year.

"We didn't try telling them about the troll. We just got the hell out of there.

"That was it."

Analysis

The machine rendered our session somewhat unusual. Garrett addresses the problem: "You can't see me on the tape recorder, but I'm shining the light all over the place." Nevertheless the troll tale's content remained unchanged from the first time I had seen and heard it performed.

I asked my guest to describe some of the feelings associated with his nocturnal visitor.

He replied, "As I said, the troll was hair-raising, but I never felt in threat of my life. Maybe I would have, if the tent had been closed and I wouldn't have been able to get out. Then it would have been different.

"But even while I was staring at the thing, part of me was saying, 'I'm seeing something cool. I am seeing something most people are never going to see. This is a supernatural creature, and I'm looking at it.'

"And it was thrilling. After I got out of the tent and looked around, I was exhilarated. And the next morning, I was still excited. I felt though that the vibe I got from it was mischievous. It wasn't evil."

He also talked about two motifs his troll shared with illustrations: "Think about all the folklore across northern Europe. Things like this are commonly portrayed as being short and having pointy ears. All legends have a basis in fact. Compare the art of Arthur Rackham to that of John Bauer, and you will see many similarities."

Two Rackham illustrations appear in *The Encyclopedia of Fairies* by Katharine Briggs. These tiny beings have long, pointed ears, hands, and feet. They lack hair.

Garrett provided a copy of *John Bauers Sagovarld* (John Bauer's World of Stories). Bauer's trolls vary in size from small to gigantic. They have orangutan eyes, long hands, long hair, furry arms, and bowed backs. Male trolls' beards nearly cover their torsos. Some have noses that resemble duck bills, which are either flat or ridged in the middle.

I asked Garrett if his troll mirrored any of those depicted by the Swedish artist. My informant replied, "No, these are human embroidering of nature spirits. They're manifestations of the earth's life force that can take on humanoid appearance."

Nature is the principal connection between those pictures. Both artists show their subjects in sylvan or rustic settings, such as seated under tree roots.

Garrett likes the art and literature associated with these creatures, but had always hoped they would live up to his credo, "All legends have a basis in fact." He pointed out an inconsistency in his own troll tale: "Although I felt the fur of the troll, it didn't leave any footprints. Whatever they are, they're only semi-corporeal. They're not completely in our plane, which would also go along with a lot of the myths."

My informant's lore also matches other folktales. Like pre-industrial believers, Garrett restricts his adventure to the periphery. Folklorist Thomas DuBois explained that "Supernatural events take place at the edge. Forests, moors, mountains, the sea, foreign lands, and cities are dangerous." Geographical edges were only one realm of danger. Night, seasonal changes, and adolescence have equal hazards.

Some of these elements apply to Garrett's stories. He and Holly camped between a lake, some trees, and an unpaved parking lot with a street lamp. It was the border between a technological society and the natural world. The campground was closed. They were alone in a foreign country, near the autumnal equinox. Night fell. The hero and heroine were nineteen and eighteen, respectively; at the threshold of adulthood. The setting was ideal for a magical visitation.

It might sound inappropriate to refer to Garrett and Holly in heroic terms. The narrator's admission of fearing a four-foot-tall troll belies his own physical strength. At the time, Garrett was an ex-football player with a massive, square-shaped frame, thick limbs, a circular face, and large, round eyes that nearly glowed in the dark. The troll frightened him because it should not have been real. Its incursion challenged modern concepts of reality. Despite Garrett's self-effacement, he still comes across as courageous. He considered his options, made a plan, surmounted terror, faced the unknown, and resigned himself to his fate.

Rules changed after the troll's escape. Garrett was now in control. He did not defer to Holly. His explanation was the accepted explanation; he favored his theory over hers, and he concocted the strategy for dealing with any further harassment. The troll no longer intimidated him.

Not every listener accepts his assessment of the intruder as a supernatural creature. "Scoffers" tag the troll as a raccoon, fox, lynx, or great horned owl. Garrett tells these people, "It doesn't matter if you don't believe me. I saw it." We will revisit the issue in the next chapter.

He sets forth that his own sincerity has convinced many skeptics. They see that he believes in the lore, and are therefore more inclined to take it seriously. Besides, he says, "I would have embellished a lie. I would have described the troll's glowing, red yes; or I'd have said I grabbed it by the tail, and flung it around the tent."

Interestingly enough, print media affected Garrett's interpretation more than electronic media. His only allusion to the latter is "Spock ears" in the troll description. This reference to the popular *Star Trek* icon gives the audience a common visualization. No other television program or movie comes up. Folktales and illustrations influenced his explanation of the event.

Print media also enhances presentation, because Garrett merges oral storytelling with short story writing. The troll tale earned him an A in a Seattle Central Community College composition course. Unfortunately, he lost the written version. Garrett also penned fantasy courses for University of Washington creative writing classes.

These skills carry over into oral performances. He does not concentrate solely on action sequences, or the supernatural, but grounds his tale in real life. Garrett describes the surroundings, develops characters, tells listeners how he felt, uses foreshadowing, and builds suspense. By that time, listeners have accepted so much of the narrative that the apparition seems like a logical outcome. Our informant tells the tale to entertain an audience, but he still believes in it. Style and sincerity combine in his story of confrontation with the supernatural.

Concrete imagery also makes the tale vivid and believable. A week after the performance, I glanced up during a downpour and noticed rain falling through a street light's glow. The sight reminded me of the raindrops which fell through Garrett's flashlight beam during his search for the troll.

As for his former girlfriend, many listeners wonder why they broke up after sharing a magical adventure.

"Traveling together is gonna make or break any relationship," Garrett explained. "It broke us. But it was an amicable divorce. We remained friends."

He used the word divorce figuratively.

Holly later married a writer for *Backpacker* magazine, and moved to Issaquah, Washington. Considering Holly's prominence in the troll tale, I wanted to hear her version of the incident.

The story has returned to Sweden. Garrett's friend, and fellow tradition bearer Ingrid Selfors Svensson tells the troll tale on rare occasions "when after-dinner conversation turns to ghost stories."

My legend trip to Lake Yngern took place in 2006. I stood out on a boulder in the water while icy November winds stabbed through my jacket and sweatshirt.

The story also had an effect on another author. Robert M. Goldstein wrote a travelogue called *Riding with Reindeer*, about bicycling the length of Finland. Mr. Goldstein spent a spooky night in a deserted cabin by a lake near the village of Suomassalmi, during a windy rain squall. He listened to some unseen intruder rifle through his bags in the dark, while branches or something else scraped at the roof. Mr. Goldstein never learned what had searched his bag, without taking anything. He also never knew what clawed aggressively at the roof, considering he couldn't find branches within thirty feet of the cabin. The storm and unknown presence reminded Mr. Goldstein of what happened to Garrett and Holly in Sweden. He hopped on his bike and peddled away.

It was an honor for us to have "The Troll Tale" cited in another writer's book.

Thanks to Ingrid Svensson and Robert Goldstein, the tale has already evolved from a memorat to a legend.

Figure 1 Carved Norwegian Troll

A carved Norwegian troll, purchased by Alma Birkedahl in Norway, 1964. It resembles Garrett Vance's description of the tent intruder in "The Troll Tale", except for the hat.

Chapter 2
The Poltergeist Story

by Garrett Vance & Holly Luidl
With Birke Duncan

An Introductory
Editorial about
Editing Transcriptions

The following chapter will take up with Garrett's

sequel to his Swedish adventure, and then examine

corroboration with his former girlfriend, Holly Luidl

Wyatt. We will expand upon many of the same themes

from the first chapter, such as the concept of the perilous

periphery, the effects of drama on oral storytelling, and the

literary influence on a raconteur. Readers will then learn

about the naturalist theory and the experience-centered

folk belief theory.

Once again, I have opted to edit transcripts because

Garrett wanted it that way in the first place. He was

annoyed by the inclusion of redundancies in the original

Northwest Folklore article. I agree with him. Unedited

transcriptions preserve some authenticity of a given

performance. Then again, the interviews in a cramped apartment were not representative of his usual performance setting. Unedited transcriptions are maddening when you read them in print. Hesitations, repetitions, and vocal false starts are the equivalents of cross outs, typographical errors, and proofreading symbols on paper. They are not artistic. It is unfair to the speaker to leave them in.

I should also explain how this chapter came about. The simple fact is that we did not have enough space to print it in that particular *Northwest Folklore* issue. This means I have to do some backtracking.

On January 26, 1996, I sat down to coffee with Garrett in the By George cafeteria, located underneath the Odegaard Undergraduate Library on the University of Washington campus. I asked him a few questions about the troll tale, and one of his statements surprised me. It turned out that on the same European jaunt in 1984, he and Holly had also met a poltergeist. Before Garrett could launch into the tale, I held up my hand and said, "No. Save it for later."

I needed an audiotape of a fresh performance.

As mentioned in the previous chapter, I met Garrett on January 31, 1996, and we recorded the troll tale in my apartment. After we concluded the story, my guest turned off the tape recorder and we took a brief break. A conversation about a ne'er-do-well acquaintance distracted us for several minutes, but we soon got back to the task at hand. Garrett turned on the machine and told the story. The following, as per the narrator's request, is an edited transcription. I have also changed the names of Holly's relatives.

"The Poltergeist Story"

"Another odd thing happened to us on this trip. This trip was full of odd things. As you know, I managed to break my bike, so we sent those things home in a box. I would have thrown mine into the bottom of the lake, but Holly insisted. She wanted to keep hers, so it cost the same to ship two as it did one. I threw mine in. It still hangs in the rafters of my boathouse, with its little shipping tags on the handlebars. I never tried to fix it, I can tell you that much. Ha, ha, ha. The cursed bike! Maybe someday I'll melt it.

"Anyway, we didn't get Eurail passes, but we did get these long-distance rail tickets. We didn't even get to Norway. We took the train to Karlstad, stayed with a friend there, then we went to Gothenburg or Goteborg, or whatever they call it. From there, we went down through Germany on the trains; the luxury of trains; the wonderful, beautiful luxury of trains. Oh, it was nice.

"We started in Hamburg, we went down to Sella, we did the *Romantische Strasse*, and ended up in Munchen. Holly had relatives there: her father's first cousins. This was a woman, who was about fifty-five years old; and her husband who happened to be some bigshot in Bavarian music. He was really cool. He always wore Lederhosen. His wife was really kooky. For some reason, he couldn't drive, so she had to. She had learned to drive when she was forty, so she was horrendous. I was in fear the whole time I was there, because I was afraid I might have to ride with her. There we were, going through the Austrian Alps, and I was in tears, cowering in the back seat. Heh, heh, heh!

"Back to the story: we're staying in that house. And also in that house is Elise. She is their thirty-year-old un-married daughter; very nice woman; very friendly. She spoke good English. But she was kind of a plain Jane. She was different. Elise was a musician, too. She played in a band. But she was very conservative, a real homebody. She didn't go out or anything which, of course, I thought was unhealthy. I think I recommended that she drink more beer. Heh, heh, heh. Slam at Birke!

"Anyhow, we did drink a lot of beer over there. It was nice, because in Germany, you get beer delivered to your doorstep. We'd be hanging out, I'd hear the doorbell, I'd open it up, and here would be a guy holding a case of fresh wheat bear. '*Danke schoen!* I love this country.'

"We stayed with the Werners for about two weeks. They had this kind of an odd house. It was about five stories tall. It wasn't really big around, but it was like five rooms with a spiral staircase off to the side. It was really a cool house.

"Holly and I got the top floor, which was kind of an attic. It had a peaked roof. You'd hit your head if you weren't careful. It was the guest room. They had these two little sofas for us to sleep on. There were all these kooky things like stuffed deer heads, stuffed grouse, candles, and cuckoo clocks. It was very Bavarian in this room.

"It was eerie anyway. It was made eerier by the fact that, again, I had the feeling that someone was watching us. I noticed that my Swiss Army knife kept disappearing. I would put it on the coffee table, go upstairs, have breakfast, come up, and it would be gone. I'd say, 'Holly, what did you do with my Swiss Army knife?'

"Nothing.'

"I didn't try to exact any confessions out of her this time. It was like, 'Oh, okay. Hmm.' I started to think [groan]: 'Something's up here.'

"I would find it over on the sofa, across the room. It really seemed to like the Swiss Army knife. I thought, 'This is classic poltergeist activity.'

"Holly started to notice this, too. I guess it was starting to get into her things and move them around. But we didn't care. We were having a good time. We thought, 'Oh well, you know, it can't hurt us.'

"Oh, here's another strange thing about the room. There was a short door that went into a storage space at the corner of the house; you know how the peaked roof came all the way down? It was like a little, triangular room. That door really freaked me out. It was always cold near it. Another classic sign, right?

"I felt like whatever was happening was emanating from there. I opened the door and looked around, but there was nothing but boxes. I thought, 'Why is this happening?'

"Then I realized that in poltergeist cases I'd read about in the past, they take place in homes where there's a troubled daughter who's going through puberty or something. They either release this energy from the trauma, or this entity is attracted to them. What I figured was, 'Here's Elise, who obviously is sexually repressed and frustrated. She's powering this poltergeist. That's why it's here. And she's probably been like this since she was fourteen. This has been going on ever since.'

"I couldn't speak German, and she was the only one who spoke English. I tried to get a feeling if anything kooky ever happened there, but they were evasive. I got the feeling that maybe there was something. They were always like [German accent, guarded tone:] 'How was your sleep?'

"It was kind of like, 'You did sleep okay, right?' thinking that whatever it was had hassled us.

"We played it cool. We didn't tell them 'poltergeist' or anything like that. I did it once, and Auntie Frieda heard me, and was startled. I noticed that, but I kept talking about something else in English. She didn't come over to see what I was talking about. That got a reaction out of her.

"The big climax to this story was the last night we were there. I brushed my teeth in kind of a half-floor they had with a bathroom. That's all they had on that floor. Holly was behind me. She was next in line.

"I went up the spiral stairs to our room, I opened the door, and there on the slanting wall was the street lights' glow through the big, triangular windows at the peak. I saw the shadow of part of a head and shoulder, a long arm, and a hand. The hand had very, very, very long fingers that tapered to points. They looked like they would have had sharp nails. The hands were wiggling. It was like: yeeh!"

Garrett wiggled his fingers slowly.

"It was holding the hand up high, and then putting it down. I blinked, and it was gone.

"I said, 'Wuh!' I turned on the lights and charged into the room, and there was nothing there. I could just feel something had happened.

71

"I said, 'Listen, don't f——-g bother me! Go back to your little room and leave me alone. I'm not someone you want to mess with!'

"I was feeling pretty physically powerful at that point. You know [deep, dramatic voice] 'I fought with the troll in Sweden. You can't mess with me.'

"I stood in the window to see where the thing would have to be in order to cast that shadow. The shape of my hand was normal. Its shadow wasn't stretched out by the light. Whatever it was really did have extremely long fingers, and it would have been standing on my bed– heh, heh–on the couch in front of the window. That's where it would have been to get the same effect.

"I made Holly stand in the door, and we replayed it all. I was even brave enough to have her turn out the light, so she could see exactly what I saw.

"Well, she didn't. She saw my shadow. You know what I mean. We experimented with it.

"She said, 'I believe you, I believe you. Something's been messing with my stuff, and I know there is a presence here.'

"'Well, what are we going to do about it?'

"She said, 'It hasn't bothered us this far, and you told it to go away, so let's go to sleep. Forget about it.'

"It wasn't until the next day, when we were on the train to Innsbruck, Austria, that she told me the next part of the story. She said, 'Well, I didn't want to alarm you, but last night it was me that couldn't go to sleep, so I stayed up. I was lying in bed with my eyes closed and felt this presence. I opened my eyes and looked over. And right in front of the little, short door, there was a figure standing there. It was four feet tall, and it seemed like it had pointy ears—not as big as your troll, but it had pointy ears. It looked like it had really long arms. It was just standing there. I said, 'What do you want?'

"'And it disappeared.'

"So she saw it. She saw more of it than I did.

"That's it. That was the poltergeist in Unterschleissheim."

The poltergeist story has a darker mood than the troll tale. Garrett commented, "The poltergeist was a different story, but it was–oh! This is weird. The word needy just jumped into my head. The thing in Germany needed attention somehow, and was going about it in the wrong way."

Structural Analysis

Before moving on to Holly's accounts, it is useful to look at how the structure of Garrett's narrative illustrates his style. William Labov and Joshua Waletzky organized the following labels for portions of personal experience narratives:

Abstract

Orientation

Complication of Action

Resolution of Action

Evaluation

Coda

The Abstract introduces the oral story by way of an undetailed summary, such as when Garrett mentioned in conversation that he and Holly had seen a poltergeist. It introduced the tale to me, but I delayed the rest of the presentation. The setting would have been perfect. The cafe was relaxed and public, but unfortunately I did not keep a tape recorder on my person.

Orientation gives the background that leads up to the main action.

Complication of Action turns the situation into a story. Some element will come up that will progress directly to conflict and climax. Complication set in for Garrett when, like in Sweden, he felt as if someone spied on him in the Bavarian attic.

Resolution of Action consists of the climax and its aftermath.

Evaluation explains the point of the story. Garrett combined Evaluation with Complication because he could already make an educated guess about the mysterious occurrences' causes.

The Coda is the final tag that concludes the tale.

Orientation, Complication of Action, and Resolution of Action constitute the narrative core. Typically, Complication outlasts Orientation. The sheer length of the latter helps to underscore a point in the first chapter, that Garrett grounds his tales in real life.

It also re-emphasizes the literary nature of Garrett's narratives. Most supernatural legends and memorats are not literary; they tend to focus completely on the supernatural event. It is definitely the case in such excellent folk narrative collections as *Ghosts Along the Cumberland* by William Lynwood Montell and *Scandinavian Folk Belief and Legend* by Reimund Kvideland and Henning Sehmsdorf. The chief benefit to such short narratives is that they are easy to transcribe.

Further analysis would have been incomplete without input from the other witness. I wrote to Holly after obtaining her address from Garrett. It would have been ideal to interview her in person, but she lived with her husband and child in Issaquah, a long way from my residence in Poulsbo, on the Kitsap Peninsula.

My letter to Holly gave her the choice of how to get back to me: telephone, letter, or email. She opted for the latter on June 18, 1998. I have reprinted her narration as she wrote it, except that I maintained her relatives' pseudonyms:

"Troll Story"

As I remember it, we were on our way to Karlstad via Sweden's convoluted highway system in October 1984. We had spent the previous night camped by a lake (where all the wild geese nested) on someone's property. If I remember properly, she took pity on us and brought us a warm casserole...Anyway after a fitful night's sleep at best, we headed off in the rain to the next town, which appeared to have a campground not far away. Never use the bike paths in Sweden, they go nowhere!!!!!

After stopping and asking directions at a gas station and biking another hour or two, we finally approached the campground. Garrett lost his mind for a

77

minute, and decided his bike was a mountain bike, and completely destroyed the derailleur going cross-country. So we pushed our bikes the rest of the way. We arrived at the campground to discover it was locked and closed. Having no choice, we set up camp in what appeared to be a sheltered spot between three old growth fir trees. (Mind you I was in a terrible mood because all I wanted was a hot shower.) Garrett was trying to be cheerful, and set about the task of making dinner out of who knows what. I think it may have been yeast. The evening turned out to be nice …clear and cool, but we were warm enough, so we spent the early evening exploring the grounds and sitting around our camp stove, drinking tea.

Then the weather changed…with dusk came the storm clouds and wind followed quickly by pelting, icy rain. We bailed for the tent, crawled into our sleeping bags (fully clothed for warmth) and went to sleep. I am a very sound sleeper, so I did not wake up until after I had to pee…really badly. I remember Garrett was freaked out about something, and wanted me to wait until morning. I uttered something not entirely nice to him as I crawled out the tent flap. He drove me crazy the whole time I was outside by shining a flashlight around and talking to me. When I returned, I was cold and tired and the tent had begun to leak. The foot of my sleeping bag was wet, and I was thoroughly disgusted. I was climbing back into my sleeping bag with my back to Garrett, when he yelled something about me pinching him...I wasn't even touching him. At this point it is very important to note that I am a rather linear person...I could have been thoroughly freaked out by this but I was cold, tired, uncomfortable, and I just wanted to survive until morning, so I went back to sleep. I was awakened a while later by Garrett jumping around in the tent (it was a very small tent) and something had stepped on my calf or foot. I began to sit upright and yell at Garrett when something brushed past my back and out of the tent. I had forgotten to close the fly when I returned from my earlier potty trip. At that point, we actually had very few words to say to each other...triage mode I think. We zipped up the tent fly, got back into our sleeping bags, put our backs together, and went to sleep.

The next morning there were no footprints around the tent except for the ones I made during my potty trip…I don't think we discussed this experience fully for about two days. I do remember Garrett telling me about hearing voices outside of the tent, and later describing the silhouette of the "thing." His description was disturbing…bipedal, furry, pointy eared.

I must admit that I am a bit of a pragmatist, and usually a hard sell on the "supernatural" experience thing, but I am convinced that whatever was in our tent that night was not simply wildlife or a figment of our imaginations.

Recalling this memory, even after all these years, still freaks me out a little.

"Poltergeist Tale"

This one is a little sketchy in my memory…however, if I remember correctly, I believe I was the one who saw this one…We were staying at my Aunt Frieda and Uncle Johannes's house in

Unterschleissheim just outside of Munich. It was a typical European house with small dark rooms and narrow staircases…and a mysterious door. We had been there for a while and had heard some mysterious bumpty bumpty in the night. When we questioned my Auntie about this and mentioned Poltergeist, she became quite silent…a state-of-being very foreign to her…odd because we had been doing the youth hostel thing for a while and were both quite anal about keeping our stuff organized. The details up to the sighting are foggy, but I think it was our last night, and I woke up late from a sound sleep, and saw a small dark figure in our room…which subsequently disappeared when I woke Garrett up and turned on the light…Did the troll follow us?!!?

Hope this helps.

Holly.

Analysis

Email and letter writing are an easy way to record the text of a story. One gets a sense of the narrator's style, humor, and personality, but this method lacks the dramatic immediacy of personally seeing and hearing a tale's performance.

Though their memories diverge in some respects, the narrators' versions are fairly close. Garrett remains the pivotal character, and their characterizations of him are consistent. Nature also remains vital to both versions of the troll tale.

This is an important motif. The naturalist folk belief theory, from the nineteenth century, maintained that natural features looked super natural to human perception. Fairies represented everything dangerous and wild about nature.

That does not mean that living in a modern, urban setting eliminates magical thinking. International Law attorney Jennifer Foss informed me that city dwelling Russian citizens of the Soviet Union believed quite literally in ghosts and curses, despite insulation from rural life. Ghost and household spirit belief is also normal in modern, urbanized Japan.

We should also remember Garrett's sensation of being watched at a campground, preceding a storm. A skeptic might attribute his discomfort to a drop in barometric pressure. The ominous cloud bank and storm overwhelmed Garrett and Holly for obvious reasons, and left them powerless.

The connection of magical creatures to nature remains topical. French folklorist Virginie Amilien points out that late twentieth century Norwegian culture portrayed the troll as an ecological guardian or "environmental helper." Garrett's beliefs relate to that continuity.

In Holly's version, as with Garrett, one sees how the two young people have placed themselves at the perilous periphery. Pre-industrial beliefs maintained that one was most likely to meet the supernatural in that unprotected area.

Lauri Honko's article "Memorates and the Study of Folk Belief" points out that violation of a norm can provoke an alleged supernatural experience. The perilous periphery comes across as an emotional state brought on by a loss of control over a situation. These elements apply to the troll tale. In both accounts, Garrett sabotaged his girlfriend's planned activity by breaking his bicycle. They violated another norm by camping out of season.

This is also a case where obeying a norm added to their troubles. Threat assessment expert Gavin De Becker asserts that people are socially conditioned to rationalize their intuition away, and deny subconscious warning signals, even in life threatening situations. When Garrett ignored feelings of being watched and failed to alert Holly, he left himself open to attack.

Readers of Garrett's account will remember his planned use of the Swiss Army knife to fight the troll. This is also consistent with folk beliefs. Knives were said to protect one from evil spirits. That is Motif E 434.7 "Knives as protection from revenants", from Stith Thompson's influential motif-index.

The theft of the couple's bread, not mentioned by Holly, is also significant. Another great folklorist,

Katharine Briggs said that bread ordinarily wards off fairies and other sinister supernatural creatures. However, Briggs maintains that bread can also serve as an offering to magical beings, such as Pwca, the tricky Welsh version of the English Puck. That scenario meshes with Garrett's portrayal of the troll as mischievous, not malevolent.

Both accounts convey how Holly and Garrett's stay in the campground felt. Garrett emphasizes dread turning to terror. Holly focuses on discomfort and aggravation. The supernatural part of the story starts and ends quickly for Holly, whereas Garrett describes a suspenseful standoff.

Readers should also note the narrators' different resolutions after the being's escape. Garrett recalls a dialogue wherein he convinces Holly that their visitor was a troll. She, on the other hand, remembers going back to sleep and not discussing the adventure fully for two days.

Holly is an experienced camper, hiker, farmer, and veterinary assistant. She makes a point that their visitor was probably neither animal nor imaginary. An intrusive lynx, canine, raccoon, or owl would have to have regarded humans as non-threatening, since it boxed itself in at the back of the tent, with humans blocking the only escape route. Both narrators mention that the visitor left no footprints in the mud; but Holly points out that she herself left tracks from the night before. A dog, raccoon, or lynx would have left paw prints. Holly would have then pointed out the evidence to Garrett, and they could have laughed off the experience as a mistake.

One remaining animal suspect would be a great horned owl or close European relative, considering the tufted ears and lack of footprints. However, those avians are not four feet high and covered with hair. They do not grow larger than two-and-a-half feet tall. These nocturnal birds of prey avoid humans. Joining Garrett and Holly in a small tent seems unlikely.

Many listeners have brought up those animal theories to Garrett. It shows that skepticism requires a great deal of creative thought, for the visualization of scenarios. This book will study mistaken perceptions of the supernatural in the chapter "Four Anti-Memorats."

The journey continued, as did the issue of the perilous periphery. Garrett and Holly visited another foreign land and slept in an attic. The poltergeist concentrated in a corner of the marginal room. It also reportedly interfered with Garrett's access to his knife. If we take the story too seriously, then we would consider this a preventive strike on the part of the poltergeist, since a knife could conceivably hurt it. As if to underscore "the edge" the apparition did not visually reveal itself until the last night of Garrett and Holly's visit.

Once again, Garrett describes an incomplete picture of a supernatural being. Street lights aided his vision both times. Considering his involvement in amateur theater, he knew the dramatic power of simple lighting and shading techniques. This knowledge complements his knack for description. He describes the images so well that at times, when listening to him or reading his stories, one feels as if one were watching a film.

Garrett and Holly believed in what they saw. In his version, they worked together to explain the mysterious image, and arrived at a supernatural conclusion. The accounts differ on the Resolution of Action.

Holly puts a different spin on the end of the poltergeist story. It raises the possibility that the apparition arose from the narrators themselves, and not the place they visited. A symbolist would argue that the troll and poltergeist are a manifestation of the couple's deteriorating romance.

Why do their accounts of the troll tale dovetail more closely than their versions of the poltergeist story? Garrett explained this factor two years before I contacted Holly. He said that they told the troll tale together in a pub, also to one of Holly's cousins, and in other settings. His former girlfriend admits to not remembering the poltergeist incident as clearly as the Swedish adventure. She does not mention Elise, who Garrett considers to be central to the poltergeist activity. Even so, like her old boyfriend, Holly captures the spooky mood of the Bavarian house.

These stories do not prove the existence of the supernatural, but they give insight into why people would hold such beliefs. The experience-centered folk belief theory supports the sincerity of those who report supernatural events. Folklorist David Hufford defined the theory as follows: "Some significant portion of traditional supernatural belief is associated with accurate observations interpreted rationally" (xvii).

The troll tale illustrates the basic formula. Someone has a weird experience: Garrett & Holly meet something strange in their tent. They evaluate the experience through cultural sources: they are in Sweden; trolls are part of Scandinavian tradition. They tell people about it: Holly and Garrett incorporate the tales into their festive repertoires. The above affect their beliefs from then on: if this experience was real, then other experiences might be real.

Conclusion

Garrett and Holly's adventures have turned into exemplary folk entertainment. Garrett's performance is a veritable one man show, in two acts, which has traveled around the world with him. Examination of these tales introduces readers to a wide variety of folk belief theories, continuities from pre-industrial lore, and the interdisciplinary relationships of storytelling, drama and literature.

Holly Luidl, Auntie Frieda Werner, and Garrett W. Vance
in Unterschleissheim, Germany, 1984. A scene from "The
Poltergeist Story."

Chapter 3

Experiences with the Fairies;
Tradition, Imagination, & the Media

by Jason Harris

Introduction

It may come as something of a surprise to some readers to discover that Birke Duncan and I have recorded fairy lore here in the Northwest. Indeed, even Peter Narvaez in his 1997 book *The Good People:New Fairylore Essays* while contradicting Richard M. Dorson's contention that "they were not evident on this side of the Atlantic", Narvaez personally had only examples from Canada, not the United States to offer, though he interviewed informants in both countries. Janet Bord, however in her book *Fairies: Real Encounters with Little People*, does present recent accounts of encounters in the United States. Regardless, it came somewhat as a surprise to find memorats involving fairies among our informants. The fairy memorates were far more detailed, and there were twice as many as UFO accounts.

After comparing our informants' testimonies (see below for transcripts) on "little men" and fairies, we find that theories of Carl Sagan and other watchdogs of superstition need revision. We recorded four accounts detailing the physical appearance of fairies, which are included here.

Sagan proposes in his book *The Demon-Haunted World: Science as a Candle in the Dark* that the fairy faith of yesteryear is a relic of the past and is merely the antiquated manifestation of a mechanics of belief that is producing the mania in aliens that is growing today:

"Perhaps everyone knows that gods come down to Earth, we hallucinate gods; when all of us are familiar with demons it's incubi and succubi; when fairies are widely accepted, we see fairies; in an age of spiritualism, we encounter spirits; and when the old myths fade, we begin thinking that extraterrestrial beings are plausible, then that's where our hypnagogic imagery tends" (131).

While Sagan's hypothesis may be true in regard to the mechanics of dreams–that we fantasize on those

93

subjects which are represented broadly in our culture as credible–he simplifies the range of belief in our society. It is not the case that demons and spirits have departed from the belief systems of people, or their imaginations.

While we are poised to enter the twenty-first century [as of 1999, when this chapter first appeared] that does not mean modern culture has wholly abandoned traditions of the past. Medieval and even truly ancient beliefs coexist in people's minds with the knowledge that we have sent spacecraft into outer space and are developing the technology of cloning. The code that ostensibly governs many people's morality and spiritual beliefs is founded upon the Bible. The priority given to what amounts to a primitive system of belief is a testament to the fact that modern society incorporates a variety of disparate beliefs–material far removed in time from the industrial and scientific world. The rise of multiculturalism in the United States has helped preserve different cultures and voice a variety of beliefs. African, Asian, Irish, and Jewish folklore circulate widely, to name

94

just a few compressed terms which represent incredible diversity of belief within those ethnic groups and our society at large.

When we read in the news of exorcisms that still take place and we see the incredible attention to a 1973 movie called *The Exorcist* we cannot deny that many of us if not "familiar with demons" are at least fascinated with the prospect. Furthermore, some of us do more than simply believe, and in fact cause great harm to presumed victims of demonic possession. Films, such as *What Dreams May Come*, *The Blair Witch Project*, and *The Sixth Sense* demonstrate the large degree of public interest, regardless of religious persuasion, in the supernatural. It is clear that popular culture has adapted for public consumption the mystique of what were once primarily folk and religious beliefs and rituals. Secular media has helped preserve and popularize many of the traditions of religion and folklore, though the treatment of this cultural heritage in print and on film is often imprecise, irreverent, and reductive. Beyond the silver screen, interest in spiritualism is far from absent: from psychics who prophesied disaster in the year 2000, to college students playing at Ouija boards–if not always overt belief, great interest abounds in the possibility of spiritual communications. Indeed, testimony of our informants suggests that belief in demons and spirits is far more evident than this epidemic of extraterrestrial mania which Sagan suggests is the equivalent of fairy belief of yesteryear.

By pointing out flaws with the premises in the likes of Sagan it is far from the purpose of this examination to suggest that aliens and fairies in fact exist. Rather, the motivation here is to demonstrate the belief in fairies is not extinct, regardless of the developing belief in the visitation of extraterrestrials. What is perhaps most surprising about Sean Gulager's testimony of "little men" and Ashley's report of "fairies" is that these informants present, seemingly unwittingly, two models of fairy belief: Sean's case represents a more traditional perception while Ashley's report seems more influenced by modern media.

The Interviews

Birke Duncan & I both recorded the following interviews on separate tape recorders. Birke has been the main transcriber for both sessions and thus it is he who provides the narrative voice and commentaries in the sessions. I made formatting and other editorial additions here and there, after comparing his transcriptions with my tapes, and have inserted supplementary information gleaned from subsequent chats with the informants as well.

Here, then are both interviews: Sean first, then Ashley.

#1 "The Little People"
Interview with Sean Gulager
April 9, 1999

Transcribed by Birke Duncan

Jason Harris and I interviewed Sean Gulager [pseudonym] in the Stevens Court meeting room on the University of Washington campus. At the time of our conversation, he was finishing up his first year of a Master of Sciences program in fisheries.

Sean was born on July 14, 1976, and raised in the small town of Douglas, Georgia. He has a sister, five years his senior, and a brother five years his junior.

Jason: Was anything haunted?

Sean: I never believed the house was haunted. No.

Jason: What unusual tale might you tell about your house?

Sean: Well, when we moved into the house, it seemed very weird. I just remember what my parents said. There was no vegetation in the yard, and everything in the house was green, including the walls and carpet. And it

98

seemed very strange, so immediately my parents decided, "We have to do something about this." We planted a lot of trees. They made more colors. It's funny, because green is my favorite color now.

Jason: At some point, you realized there was something else in the house, perhaps?

Sean: Well, I remember as a child maybe seeing little characters that walked around the house. These things would just disappear, walk through, and sort of not see me, but I would see them. I wasn't afraid of them or anything. No one else in the house seemed to see them.

Jason: What age were you when you saw them?

Sean: I would say maybe seven or eight. It wasn't like a one-time thing; it was often. I was never surprised when they walked through. I just kind of accepted it.

Birke: How tall were they?

Sean: They were about three feet high. I would always see males–they would always be male. They seemed to be very mature, and older.

Jason: How old did they seem to be?

Sean: It's kind of hard to age them. They seemed to be human, but not human at the same time. If you know what I mean. I don't know, I never really thought about how old they were. But if I did put an age on them, they would be older because their faces seemed to be wrinkled.

Jason asked if they had any other distinguishing characteristics.

Sean: Long hair. It was light in color, like grayish or dark brownish...a strange color; a dark grayish color almost like this table top. It's not a color you see every day. They looked like normal humans. They weren't White or Black; they seemed to be some kind of tannish, off-color. You don't see people with this sort of facial texture, which seemed to be hard, or thick, or rough. It didn't look smooth.

I asked about the distance between the little people and Sean.

Sean: Maybe always like five feet or something like that. They never really acknowledged me as being present. I never called out to them directly. They would always seem to be doing something, and I didn't really know what they were doing. They would always walk into the room, walk out, and not look at me.

I asked if anyone else had seen them.

Sean: No one else in my family saw them. But recently my little nephew has started to see them. This was quite a surprise to me because I was home for break. We were all sitting in the den. He comes in–he calls my mother Nana–and he says, "Nana, there are these little (--I don't remember the exact words he used for them–) things back there walking around." Immediately, she dismissed it as false or fictitious. I was thinking [Gasp!]: "I saw these things, now he's seeing them." He's six now, but he was maybe five, I believe, when he first started seeing them. And he's afraid of them. Now he's afraid to go back there by himself.

Jason asked if Sean wanted to talk to his nephew about them.

Sean: No.

Jason: You don't want to?

Sean: No, I mean why would I? It just seems like something not even worth talking about.

Jason: Do you think you could learn something about them from him?

Sean: It's not like something I'm trying to see; something that really is of curiosity for me. I'm not trying to search for the truth about it.

Birke: When was the last time you saw them?

Sean: Well, maybe the latter part of my teenage years but only at the side of my vision. I don't recall seeing them straight on, like when I was smaller. If I saw them now, it wouldn't surprise me. It would be like a bird flying in the sky.

Birke: Were they always the same individuals?

Sean: Yes. I remember two or three; never more than that. They never interacted with each other. I don't remember what they were doing. They were doing something. It wouldn't all be one at a time.

Birke: What kind of clothes were they wearing?

Sean: They were wearing what I would call maybe "medieval period." They wore big clothes that weren't really fitting and not anything that would be strange today but primarily they were natural colors, like green and orange. They always wore berets straight on top of their heads. I want to say the hats were green, but I don't remember the color.

Jason: What would you classify these as, if you had to?

Sean: Little people.

Jason: [snicker]: Little people.

Birke: Makes sense.

Jason: Before, you used the word trolls. I was wondering why you chose that word.

Sean: Well before, I remember as a kid seeing this movie one night called *Troll*. These things reminded me of trolls. In the movie, trolls were evil. I mean, I never called them trolls before, but they seemed to resemble trolls in this movie. *Troll* is a movie I was very afraid of.

Jason: Did you have a doubt about the little people?

Sean: I wasn't afraid of them, but in the movie you should be afraid of them because they would hurt you.

Jason asked if any other strange occurrences took place in the home.

Sean: Well, I remember in my bedroom there were some strange occurrences. This one particular day, something happened with this whole chester; a chest of drawers. It had belonged to my grandmother, and we'd had it redone. It has these five drawers. It's huge, and heavy to move. It got moved across to the other side of the room one day. And no one knew anything about it. That is still a mystery to this day.

Jason: Did you guys talk about it?

Sean: Yes, I questioned everyone about it. Why would this happen? It was just an unexplained event. And the door to my room would open and close without me doing it myself. I would always sleep with my door open at night. I'd wake up in the morning, and my door would be closed. I'd ask my parents about it. "Oh, we didn't close it." Nobody closed my door. I would always take naps in the afternoon. The door would be open. "Someone's been here."

Jason: Have you ever seen a ghost or anything like that?

Sean: No, I've never seen a ghost, but I've felt that some spirit was there, in my house.

Jason: How did that happen?

Sean: Well, I would hear someone call my name a lot; and also hear footsteps like someone walking at night through the house.

Jason: Do you know who that might have been?

Sean: I just assumed it was my grandfather. He died when I was in the sixth or seventh grade. Then I remember after that, someone would call my name. I just assumed it was him. My sister also experienced this.

Jason: Oh? Was it the exact same thing?

Sean: Yeah, except her name.

Jason: Did it sound like your grandfather's voice, or does it sound like an undistinguishable male voice?

Sean: It sounded like a male voice. I can't recall exactly what my grandfather's voice sounded like. Before he died, he had a stroke. He didn't talk like he normally would, and that went on for five years. I mean, I was just too young to know what his voice sounded like when he was walking, and well.

Birke: How long after his death did you hear his voice?

Sean: I would say maybe a year and a half, or two years. It wasn't immediate. When I heard this voice, I would ask other people, like my mother: "Did you call me?" They'd say, "No." The only reason I associate it with my grandfather is because of my sister. She heard her name and she thought it was Granddad calling her. I assumed the same thing.

Jason: Right. You never mentioned the little people to your family members?

Sean: Oh, yeah. Everyone in the family is well aware that I've seen these little people.

Jason: No one believes you, though.

Sean: No. No one believes me.

Jason: Your sister doesn't believe you.

Sean: No, she's a school psychologist, and she believes it's something going on in my head. [Sean laughs]

Jason: Does she know about your nephew, too?

Sean: Yeah. He's her son.

Jason: She doesn't think anything of that.

Sean: No.

Jason: Have you ever seen anything else that might qualify as a little out of the ordinary? Have you had a supernatural or spiritual experience?

Sean: Not that I can really think of.

Jason: Did you ever think you were saved by an angel? Some people talk about that, like if they were in an auto accident where they should have died.

Sean: No.

Jason: Out of body experience?

Sean burst out laughing.

I turned off my tape recorder and explained, "He's reaching now. Jason has had a lot of success with making people remember other stories."

I wanted Jason to hurry up because Sean had to get to a class at 11:30. My position at the table gave me a clear view of Jason's digital watch. My collaborator had his left hand on the table, with the display upside down. It read 11:15. I brought up the time.

Jason said, "This is fast, by the way, in case you glanced at it. I always keep it twenty-five minutes ahead, so that I'm never really late."

That, on its own, was an uncanny experience.

Jason continued the interview:

Jason: How did the little men and hearing the ghost fit into your beliefs about the world, nature, God, and that kind of thing?

Sean: I don't think that the experiences when I was back home influenced my life in any way. I can't make any associations. Recently I've become this very spiritual, radical Christian.

Jason: What do you mean by radical?

Sean: Today I'm a very spiritual person who believes in one God, and that God being the God in the Bible; and Him having the power over my life. I believe everything in the Bible and try to incorporate the Bible into my everyday life.

Jason: Do you keep the little men and the ghost separate?

Sean: Well, I don't see those things in conflict with my religion. I really don't question it, and I don't really understand it. It's just something that's been part of me and something I'm not really even concerned with figuring out.

Jason: How many people have you told these stories to?

Sean: I really don't share the story about the little men too often. This is the first time I've talked about it with people outside of my immediate family. I share the story of my grandfather occasionally. It's common with a lot of people. They believe that spirits or people from their past interact with them today. Recently, I shared the story with someone I met out at North Bend. He's an anthropologist who's interested in this for some reason. It's not something I'm ashamed of, because it's common. I don't think it's really unusual.

Jason: Did anyone ever tell you a "little men" story?

Sean: Well, when people say "little men" they usually associate that with aliens, UFOs, things out of this world. I really don't know much about fairies. When I've thought of fairies, I always think about things that fly. I don't think they were angels. I think with an angel, you'd have interaction with them. They [the little men] would come anytime. They would have to come from somewhere, but I would never think of where they were coming from. Whenever they would leave, they would go out from the room into the hallway.

Epilogue

Explaining his religious beliefs, Sean mentioned how a friend thought he was in a cult, because of the thoroughness with which he integrated religion into his life. The friend also raised the issue that Sean should not believe in dinosaurs if he believes everything in the Bible. This gave Sean some pause: "I will have to figure out if I truly believe dinosaurs ever existed."

Regarding cults, it is intriguing to note that Sean later told Jason Harris something. Sean's parents had heard there actually was some sort of cult which had previously owned their property. Sean did not know any other details than that.

We soon wrapped up the session, put our chairs back against the wall, and packed up our tape recorders.

Sean said to us, "Thanks for not laughing at me. Maybe you'll laugh when I leave."

We both laughed when he said that.

#2 "Fairies and Angels"
Interview with Ashley Morris
January 22, 1999

Transcribed by Birke Duncan

Ashley Morris [alias] was born on April 9, 1977, in Seattle. She earned her B.A. in French Language & Literature in June of 1999.

At the time of our meeting, Ashley took a break from filling out an application. She later earned an M.A. in teaching. Ashley's interests included yoga, swing dancing, and historical fiction. She plays such instruments as piano and flute, and performed in the UW Huskies' marching band at sporting events.

The following interview took place at 10:45 a.m. on January 22, 1999, in the ground floor lounge of Hansee Hall. Jason and I set up our tape recorders on the coffee table.

Jason said, "Go for it, but first:" He pulled out a camera, aimed it at our informant and said, "Hey, Ashley. Click."

She looked left and snapped the picture a few inches from her face.

Ashley said, "Jason! What was that for?"

"I had it along. Maybe we'll use it. It's all right. You weren't in your bathroom."

Ashley laughed. She asked me, "Is this going to be me recounting my story, or do you have questions?"

"Questions later," I replied.

Jason added, "We have ways of making you talk."

After she stopped laughing, Ashley began her narrative. "Let's see. It was in the summer of 1984. I was seven years old and I was at Camp Robbinswold which is located on the coast of Washington. I don't remember what town it's in, or what it's by, but it's a girl scout camp."

Camp Robbinswold is on the west side of the Hood Canal, near the town of Lilliwaup on the Olympic Peninsula, on the east side of the Olympic National Park.

"I was there for a week-long girl scout adventure type-thing. It was probably either the third or fourth night

I was there. I was in my cabin on the upper bunk. I woke up and looked over my head. There were two images floating across the room. They had come in from the door. They didn't have faces. They were very small, probably two or three inches high. They both had gowns on. One was pink and one was blue. They both had golden hair, but there were no faces. It was just kind of a blob of beige or cream or whatever you want to call it. The one in pink had kind of a stick in her hand, with a gold star on the end. They floated above my head. I thought at first that I was dreaming. I turned my head and blinked several times, to make sure that I wasn't hallucinating. They drifted out of the window, and I never saw them again. That was basically it."

There had been three other girls in the cabin, but Ashley told none of them. It was turned into a cherished secret, because she felt privileged to have witnessed the event. Besides that, the other kids might have laughed.

Ashley didn't start telling the story until a few years later. Not many people believed her anyway, so she rarely brought it up. Jason asked if Ashley had told her mother. Our informant replied, "I don't remember if I told my Mom or not. She probably just would have smiled and said, 'Oh, that's nice.'"

I asked, "What do people usually say when they hear it?"

"They just give me an odd look and say, 'Oh, sure.'"

Jason asked about how Ashley thought fairies fit into the grand scheme of things. She had to give the question more thought. My colleague followed up with: "Are fairies more like ghosts, angels, or something in between?"

"I've seen angels."

"Oh, I didn't know that. What was the occasion?"

"I was sleeping in my bed. I don't remember how old I was; maybe ten or eleven. I woke in the middle of the night, and I looked at the end of my bed. There was a band of angels, six of them, with their heads bowed. They weren't very big, but bigger than the fairies.

Jason: Could you see their faces?

Ashley: They had eyes. I remember that. They were dressed in white. They had golden hair. That really stayed with me. I told my Mom about that. We're both spiritual, religious people, so she believed it.

Jason: Was there any kind of event at the time where you felt you needed some faith or help?

Ashley: I don't think of anything specific, but at the time I was having some family problems with my father. I had been in touch with him briefly, when I was seven. He moved to Ohio suddenly. That was a difficult transition for me because I was a young girl, just getting to know her Dad, this hero figure, and then–all of a sudden–he leaves. I wasn't really sure how to deal with it. And that went on for years: that feeling of loss and not really knowing how to handle the situation.

Jason: That was kind of general. It wasn't like it happened the night before.

Ashley: No.

Jason: And what did you feel when you saw this?

116

Ashley: Peace. I pray a lot. I believe angels are guardians, or whatever you want to call them. I was surprised, but only initially because I believe there are forces out there to protect you whether it comes from within yourself or without. I don't know if I believe in personalized guardian angels. If there's a need in someone, it will be met.

Birke: What made you so certain they were angels?

Ashley: They looked like the stereotypical preconception of what an angel is supposed to look like, from a Western perspective. They were all very peaceful looking, very gentle, floating in the air.

Jason: Did they have wings?

Ashley: No wings.

Jason asked about the main difference between the angels and the fairies.

Ashley: The feeling was definitely different. The clothing was different, and the size.

Birke: This is happening at night each time.

Ashley: Both times were in the middle of the night, around three or four in the morning.

Birke: How can you see them so clearly?

Ashley: They're very bright figures. I guess it would be like waking up and having someone shine a flashlight in your face.

Jason: Do they cast light, or do they just light themselves.

Ashley: I would say there was a little glow around them, but it didn't radiate very far. It was just a very short distance.

Birke: What kind of light was it? Yellow? Ultraviolet? Blue?

Ashley: I would say that it was somewhere between white and gold.

Jason: Do you think there's any relation between fairies and angels?

Ashley: I would say they come from different parallels, if that makes sense. Their purpose would probably be quite different. I don't know all that much about fairies. I read the book quite some time ago. You [Jason Harris] asked me before, how I felt fairies fell into the grand scheme of things.

Jason: Right, right, right. I appreciate that. You don't have to answer. I was just asking because I didn't know about the angels.

Ashley: No, I think that's very important. Most people assume that fairies are a figment of imagination, and something that you hear from stories as a child; or cartoons or whatnot. I don't think that the reality we know, and the world we know, is the only one. I do believe that there are other universes, realities, or parallels that fairies come from. It could be on earth, or it could be in a different place, and they come here. I don't know. That's how I see it. People often get so locked into what they see that that's all they can believe, and they shut their minds off to everything else that might exist.

[Sirens from an ambulance wailed outside.]

Jason: Did you feel they were good creatures?

Ashley: Absolutely. I didn't feel in danger at all.

119

Jason: Do you think they were there to tell you something, or were you in the right place at the right time?

Ashley: I think with the fairies I was in the right place at the right time, because I didn't sense a message or anything like that. With the angels, I definitely sensed a feeling of peace, like things were going to be all right. There was a message there, even if it was unspoken.

Jason: Do you think angels are morally better than fairies?

Ashley: Not necessarily. I think they just have different roles. I personally believe that angels are Messengers of God.

Jason: Do you think people are more likely to believe the angel story?

Ashley: Absolutely. Poulsbo [Washington] is a fairly religious community. There are some pretty hardcore people out there. Of course, it's the [nineteen]nineties. Technology is kind of taking over. I guess people are looking for something to turn to. And there's that whole angel fad. Even if people aren't religious, they want to believe there's something spiritual out there to take care of them. You see angels everywhere: in calendars, books, movies, TV shows, specials. People will be far more likely to believe the story about angels because they would want to believe it.

Jason: Do you expect to see anything like this again?

Ashley: I don't know. It would be great if I did, just because it's so different from my everyday experience.

Jason: You probably believed in angels before you saw them.

Ashley: Yes.

Jason: Did you believe in fairies before you saw them?

Ashley: I'd never really thought about it. It wasn't, 'Oh, I believe in fairies, I hope I see one.'

I was so fascinated by Jason's line of questioning that I hadn't spoken in a while. This left me tongue-tied to the point where I could barely spit out the following question: "Are you more likely to believe other people's accounts of supernatural incidents?"

Ashley: Definitely. I do have a hard time swallowing: "I was abducted by aliens, and they sucked my brains out and performed medical experiments on me."

Ashley hadn't heard that from anyone she knows. She reminded us that it comes up on TV series like *The X-Files*. Nevertheless, she remains open to other people's tales of magical encounters: "I don't think I'm the one person on earth who's been able to see anything supernatural."

Jason observed, "Those are really positive experiences."

"Definitely," Ashley replied, "Absolutely. Most first person stories I've heard of ghosts are quite believable. There's no reason for me to believe that they do not exist."

Epilogue by Birke Duncan

The session broke up, since Ashley had to finish her application. I found her to be a pleasant conversationalist with an interesting point of view.

The beings in her stories had obvious similarities. Both diminutive sets of fairies and angels appeared to someone awakening at night. Ashley said that the fairies bore no resemblance to illustrations in the book, *Fairies*. Their gowns reflect the custom for dressing small children: pink for girls and blue for boys.

This interview shows the necessity of follow-up questions. They revealed yet another account of a supernatural incident, and provided insight into how the events affected Ashley's beliefs.

Analysis by Jason Harris

Let us begin our examination with Sean. I use the term "traditional" with restrictions to describe his experience. Sean claimed to have no knowledge of fairy traditions as a child, and only thought of them as "these things that fly." However, he had heard of the

123

Scandinavian troll, albeit only through exposure to media, which he associated with these "little men." Sean's description of little men has nothing in common with folkloric trolls, underground dwellers, and as regard the media representatives, other than the vague impression that his little men reminded them in appearance, Sean's little people bear far more resemblance to reports of the fairies in Great Britain.

First of all, there is the gender. Sean's little men are just that: male. And traditions of encounters with trooping fairies (which refers to more than one on some expedition or ritual), generally describes groups of male fairies.

The females are either in positions of power, which separate them from the trooping males; or are encountered in situations that entail solitary action. Examples of solitary female fairies include fairy lovers, the Banshee, or the Fairy Midwife tales–where a human woman encounters a fairy lady who asks the mortal to nurse her child.

Meetings with male fairy troops are more random in nature–unlike the clearer purposes suggested in legends often involving encounters with female fairies. Sean Gulager's encounter with two or three little people, who are all male, seems consistent with regard to these traditions. Sean is ignorant as to why the beings are there; he is a mere observer of some activity of trooping male fairies which have some business at hand in his home. Notably there are accounts of conflicts of property between fairies and humans, usually involving the location of the economic means of production or livelihood for a family. Common examples include features such as "the mill is used by fairies' ' or "the house itself may be built on fairy property"; though in Sean's case there is no overt struggle or contest, simply coexistence.

The dress of these little men, either green or orange, and the height of Sean's little people of about three feet, is fairly consistent with tradition. For instance, in certain Counties of Ireland, we find that "the fairies are generally visually conceptualized as small, and dressed in red and "green" The same is true of Welsh accounts, such as a memorate given further below, where the fairy is about a "yard" high.

While fairies have ranged from various heights in different folk narratives, the general impression of fairies has moved towards a gradual diminishing in size, as time has marched on. Generally then we do not see the giant or human-sized demigods of Celtic mythology in recent accounts, at least as far as British tradition goes–which would be the likely influence on Sean's neighborhood in the South.

Katharine Briggs emphasizes this variety of fairy sizes is a constant, rather than an evolving feature, in *The Fairies in English Tradition and Literature*: "some of our earliest fairies, the Portunes, are said by Gervase of Tilbury to be only half an inch in height." while citing additional medieval manuscripts which give examples of "child-sized fairies" and "the fairy bride of human size" (3). Yet, Briggs does not provide a section in her index for human-sized fairies, only the small ones, as though it is only the small size that is of interest.

Regardless, it is not difficult to find folk legends in Briggs's *A Dictionary of British Folk-Tales* that present human-sized fairies. These taller representatives however tend to figure within legends from Ireland and Scotland, and appear to be of noble blood–suggesting a derivation from Celtic mythological traditions. They may also perhaps be mystical doubles of aristocrats: the uncanny incarnations of feudalism, so to speak. It is telling that in Ireland the fairies are often referred to as the "gentry." Often these taller beings are not recognized as fairies, until a display of magical power reveals their nature.

Briggs also cites the influence of the "Shakespeare tradition" which supplied us with such beings as "the small flower fairies" (133). Suffice it to say then that almost any size of fairy from miniscule to man-sized has a precedent in folk tradition and medieval manuscripts. The important distinction to make is that literature from the seventeenth century onwards has tended to paint the fairies as usually small beings and that image has influenced the fairy portraiture in film today, such as Disney.

Briggs asserts that green as a fairy color as well as small size was a common observation within the prior century in Britain: "At the end of the last century the small, lively, green fairies were to be found in the North of England as well as in the South West" (133). In Ireland green and red are the fairy colors, and red is associated with magic internationally. Sean's orange may be seen as an approximation of red, though I know of no other case where "orange" is used in a description. Assuredly, it's "green" which is tempting to focus on: the green of the vegetation planted outside, the strange green carpet and paint, the green garb, which along with the orange, Sean calls "natural colors." He says: "They were natural colors, like green and orange. They always wore berets straight on top of their heads. I want to say the hats were green, but I don't remember the color." It seems of further significance that Sean expresses a desire to continue the motif of hats. Thus, there seems to be in the current of color identification a connection to the elemental view of fairies or little men as nature spirits, which we will explore further below.

Sean's attitude, which may strike a reader as surprisingly blase, is actually typical of the tone of some adherents of folk belief; they don't seek a totalizing explanation of their memorates. What is conventionally referred to as the supernatural does not properly exist in these cases, like Sean's: "If I saw them now, it wouldn't surprise me. It would be like a bird flying in the sky." Thus, the "little men" in the eyes of the informant are merely part of a larger world which can contain mysteries without its laws being violated by the appearance of what seems anomalous to non-participants in this experience.

Interestingly, there seems to be a trace of Theosophist beliefs in Sean's account. It would be interesting to know exactly what sort of cult apparently had use of the premises previously. Theosophy was an occult movement in Victorian England started by Madame

Helena Blavatsky who claimed in *Isis Unveiled* (1877) that: "Under the general designation of fairies and fays, these spirits of the elements appear in the myth, tale, tradition, or poetry of all nations" (Carol Silver, 38). Theosophists and other occultists elaborated on the systems of the Alchemists. As particularly relates to Sean's case, are the theories of fairies being caretakers of natural habitats, as Anna Kingsford asserted, a "seeress and medical doctor": "the spirits of forests, mountains, cataracts, rivers…These are the dryads, kelpies, and elves (Silver, 39)"

Beliefs that fairies are guardians of the natural world such as the views touted by Theosophists were current during the years preceding the purchase of Sean's house, at least in England as Katharine Briggs reports: "In a television programme…in 1963 there were four people who said that they believed in fairies…One of them regarded the fairies as supplying the principle of growth in plant life" (148). Perhaps Sean's parents had said more than he recollected, and his youthful imagination had incorporated details of belief in elemental spirits. Indeed, the details that begin Sean's memorate are significant: "There was no vegetation in the yard, and everything in the house was green including the walls and carpet." This suggests that a cult may very well have had an emphasis on vegetation–given the green color, the lack of vegetation in the yard may potentially be explained by lack of upkeep over the years. What is more suggestive is the following: "My parents decided, 'We have to do something about this.' We planted a lot of trees. We made more colors. It's funny, because green is my favorite color now." The introduction of vegetation into the yard serves as perhaps a causal preamble to the appearance of the "little men"-- perhaps they represent a tie between the vegetation planted outside and the green world inside the house. However, the young Sean had no idea what they were doing–what their function was. Tying these visions to the past seems appropriate since "I never saw them in the new area"--thus, these visitors appear connected to the history of the house, not any innovation, despite the vegetation hypothesis.

Sean Gulager ultimately separates his memorate from the influence of the media. He explains that he used the word "troll" in a prior description to me, simply because the "little men" resembled the trolls in the 1986 film *Troll*–though he found their characteristics, such as personality or aura, to be entirely different. Sean's "trolls" were indifferent to humanity, while the media trolls were hostile.

The moving of the drawers is an interesting feature, since it suggests further relation to Theosophist and Spiritualist beliefs, though is not overtly stated by Sean–indeed, Sean seems to have no awareness that his memorate connects to any form of traditional or occult belief. Poltergeist activity has been linked to these elemental spirits, which in the nineteenth century were aligned with fairies in Theosophist writings and with folk interpretations. Carole Silver said in *Strange and Secret Peoples*, "it was elementals or fairies who many thought created the poltergeist phenomena in which Victorians were so interested" (164). Furthermore, we find some accounts that directly correlate poltergeist activity with the disturbance of nature: thus the fairies as caretakers, or elementals, respond by harassing the trespassers.

A poltergeist case of 1907 also aroused considerable interest and again connected the phenomenon with fairies. As Andrew Lang the folklorist and psychic investigator told the tale, a farmer's house in Northern Ireland was troubled with flying stones. The neighbors believed that fairies caused the problem, as the farmer had swept his chimney with a bough of holly, and holly is "a gentle tree", that is, a tree dear to fairies. Thus, he had offended them, and the poltergeist phenomenon was their revenge (Silver, 165).

Ultimately, what can we conclude from the similarities of the memorates described by Sean and the Theosophist belief? Can Sean somehow have been indoctrinated with Theosophist theories and not realized it? Surely not. Sean's memorates are experiential rather

133

than theoretical; his narratives are examples of how perception, imagination, and abstraction might lead to an ideology like that of the Theosophists. First, we have a window here into how the anthropomorphic imagination works towards assimilating environmental features. The ambience of green–the green carpet and walls, the green factor added outside through planting of trees–is projected into a humanoid form of these little men who wear green and orange: "natural colors." The unexplained phenomenon involving moving the dresser and closing the door involve (at least as regards the dresser) great strength or, if you like, elemental power, and seems to also be connected in terms of both locale and kind with these "little men." In the logic of causation particular to the experience, the little men as visitors to Sean's room would naturally close a door on occasion perhaps, and might well move furniture around from time to time. And, given the vision itself, they might be the quick explanation for any forgotten alteration by the human inhabitants in the house.

What we have then are the imaginative roots of Theosophist theories, or any other occultist doctrines–the raw impressions that could serve as evidence for metaphysical constructs. Sean keeps his imagination limited to the level of impression. He is not interested in interpretation: "It's just something that's been part of me and something I'm not really concerned with figuring out." Thus, Sean leaves the theories for how and why to Theosophists or other pseudoscientists and metaphysicians. It is up to the folklorist to connect Sean's testimony to traditions that he does not even know of.

Clearly, the findings of folklore should be of interest to psychologists and anthropologists who are interested in learning how exactly the individual mind relates to the influences of culture and environment. The connection in this case seems to indicate a feature of the human imagination–a kind of unconscious poetry: a personifying of one's environment in a fashion that is probably not much different from the impulses that moved early humanity to animistic belief.

But were these fairies? Sean emphasizes that he didn't think these were fairies since he seems to have thought of fairies as having wings ("...these things that fly."). The image of a winged fairy is a literary one, though the fairies of folklore could fly without wings, as far as the evidence indicates, while Sean's "little men" are much closer to traditional accounts. We find the withered features of the changeling here in these "little people" of Sean's, an interesting aspect. Indeed, other fairies, other than changelings, are sometimes described as "wrinkled" as Sean's "little people." In fact, Baughman's entry in his *Type and Motif-Index of the Folktales of England & North America* for a fairy with this type of appearance is taken from Georgia, the same State which Sean's memorate is from (F239.5.[1] Fairy has brown wrinkled face, puckered like a pine knot). This is significant, because Sean emphasized the unusual facial textures, and even the color "tannish" suggests "brown": "They weren't White or Black; they seemed to be some kind of tannish off-color. You don't see people with this sort of facial texture, which seemed to be hard or thick or rough. It didn't look smooth."

Notably also, those clothes worn by Sean's little people are described by him as "medieval"--signs of a past era. Like the relation between Sean's details of these little men wearing green in an environment that has an ambience of fertility and the belief of Theosophists in elemental spirits, there seems to be a common link in imaginative vision between folk traditions of fairies and the medieval garb and withered physiognomy. What exactly is the source for Sean's perceptions is not wholly clear, yet the likeness to traditional descriptions is unmistakable.

How is Sean's memorate of the little people unlike pre-existing accounts? Well, above all, Sean has no explanation for the sightings–no reason presents itself to his mind regarding the identity or the business of these creatures. Also, his memorate serves no clear social function–the impetus for the memorate appears to be psychological rather than socio-economic or cultural.

When he calls the beings "little people" he is not referring to the tradition of fairies, as would be the case in Britain, nor does he wish to invoke the modern idea of "little men" as being extraterrestrials. Likewise, he dismisses the term "trolls" which he had used earlier because of the difference in the impression of these beings and the negative attitude represented in the media, the movie *Troll* specifically.

Normally, memorates serve some purpose and are integrated into the legendary matrix of a community—desires and anxieties of daily life find their expression on the border between civilized experience and the symbolic threat of the unknown. However, one does find some highly abbreviated accounts of fairy sightings where there is no overt explanation for why the fairy is there, such as in the Welsh memorate from July 18, 1972–the informant was a young boy of "eight or nine", just like Sean. It was recorded by Robin Gwydaf the article "Fairy Lore", on pages 178-179 of the book, *The Good People*:

"I saw a little old fellow coming from the direction of some green bushes.

"Well, it was a little less than a yard tall perhaps, that is how it seemed to me, about a yard in height. The only thing I remember clearly is that from his waist down it was green and some reddish color around his face. That's it. Green & red and a tiny little man. He didn't say anything. At first I was a little afraid. Then I wasn't afraid at all. Not at all. And I can't remember seeing him leaving. I remember him coming. I have no recollection of him leaving."

This informant's experience takes place in the woods, thus it is consistent with the idea that legends and memorates tend to be focused on interfaces between the uncivilized and civilized worlds. Timothy Tangherlini in *Interpreting Legend* offers evidence for "the interface between" the "man-made" and the "natural" in his exploration of legends and memorates where "human control" is represented by the man-made features, and implicitly, though Tangherlini does not articulate the view, the natural connotes a coded threat to civilization (131-132). This Welsh informant seems to be an example of this clash between the civilized and uncivilized. He was specifically near where "there is a little lodge, and nearby there is a circle of black trees. Inside the circle there's moss. It sounds very romantic. There were very old tree stumps. The shape is still there as it was then, before they were destroyed" (179). Thus, we find the evocation of a past era, notably a connection between an absence of vegetation and a presence as well–the dead old stumps that were "destroyed" and the moss, clearly a new recent growth. The ambience of the physical locale is not altogether different from Sean's house where there was a conspicuous absence of vegetation initially, and then a renewal. A key difference here is the circle–for circles of vegetation are traditionally gathering places for fairies– and the clear interface between the civilized, the "lodge" and the wild, "a circle of black trees."

Unlike Sean's homestead, the site of Ashley's memorate, on the other hand, does represent a definite interface between the natural and the wild. Ashley is in a cabin at summer camp in the woods–which is very similar to the situation reported by the Welsh informant. Away from home as a young child, Ashley's visitation by the fairies in the confines of her cabin suggests a blending of security and the thrill of entering a new frontier. She is individuating as a person, in effect coming of age, or at least the ritual experience of summer camp is one step in that direction, and the appearance of the fairies serves to emphasize this developmental stage in her memory. The fact these fairies enter through the door suggests a direct and wholesome attitude–it is the natural way an above board visitor would approach. An entrance through the window would seem more menacing–the exit through the window is merely marvelous: a display of their ability to fly. The visitation is gentle and befits the summer camp experience, as a pleasurable interface with the natural world rather than a period of anxiety, in this instance.

The lack of malice or even mischief associated with Sean's little people is unusual–traditionally the

141

fairies were often far from benign. Ashley's fairies, while appearing very differently from Sean's, also are not malicious. Indifference from the fairies characterizes both encounters, which is not wholly alien from tradition—at least we are not dealing with fairy godmothers, though the features of Ashley's fairies do seem to derive partly from recent media representations about fairies.

Indeed, Ashleys fairies with their wands and pink and blue dresses are more reminiscent of Disney movies than folklore. Yet, the extreme smallness of these fairies "probably about two or three inches high" is not unheard of, as Katharine Briggs's medieval report of the half-inch high fairies indicated. The garb of Ashley's fairies, while it seems influenced by the colors of Disney, is not absent from oral reports. Though blue is more often seen in Norwegian accounts of fairies, there is a memorate of a woman from 1993 in California who describes "11 tiny blue fairies perhaps one foot tall" (98). The account appears in the 1997 book *Fairies–Real Encounters with Little People* by Janet Bord.

142

Perhaps the fact that Ashley was raised in an area which has Scandinavian immigrants would be another factor in determining the blue color. Birke Duncan has emphasized that pink and blue are the colors infants are dressed in, and I would suggest that perhaps those colors' connections with infancy are part of the liminal experience of Ashley's summer camp. Being out on her own, she is saying goodbye to the more dependent aspects of childhood. Visions of her infancy greet her silently, and gently pass on. The facelessness of these fairies is unusual, and one would tend to ascribe such an appearance to the imagery of dreams, where identities are known but faces are vague.

I am including an analysis of Ashley Morris's in this chapter because the encounter is not only similar to the dynamics of her experiences with fairies, but her clear memory of her psychological and emotional state at the time suggest the therapeutic service of certain memorates. Also, Ashley's observations and thoughts about angels helps to clarify her view of the fairies–lastly, she presented both memorates to us at the same session, the angels being an added bonus, as you have read.

In terms of physical description, the angels resemble Ashley's fairies in several ways–and there is good reason for this. Since Shakespeare, literary and artistic renderings of fairies have often endowed these beings with wings, which is not only suggestive of angel iconography, but is part of a general tendency towards assimilating the spiritual beings of different cultures into a common form. The Greek Eros, or Roman Cupid, since the Renaissance has come to resemble Christian cherubs– adorable young infants rather than signifiers of unbridled desire. The Cherubim themselves in the Old Testament were often more animalistic and fiercer in aspect that modern representations of pudgy winged baby's indicate. Stephen Harris said, in *Understanding the Bible*, "the cherub…commonly has a human face (symbolizing intelligence), the body of a bull or lion (representing strength), and wings of an eagle (indicating its supernatural swiftness as God's emissary)."

144

Perhaps one reason for alteration of the Cherubim is the increase in anthropomorphic perception between the Old and New Testament; Christianity tends to personify divinity more exclusively in human form rather than including the chaotic and animalistic powers of the divine as well, which the deity emphasizes in the Book of Job, for instance. Like the fairies, cherubs and other forms of angels have clearly been sentimentalized and rendered non-threatening in their portraits.

In terms of specific physical traits, there are numerous similarities, and a few intriguing differences between Ashley's two memorates. Golden hair is a common feature of both Ashley Morris's fairies and angels, both wear gowns–white for angels instead of pink and blue for fairies–and both angels and fairies are small, though Ashley emphasizes the angels were taller–perhaps signifying their greater stature in her spiritual estimation of them. In addition the angels have no wings–despite the prevalence of wings in popular iconography of angels– while the fairies have wings. It may be that the lack of wings for the angels again suggests a degree of power, which transcends the naturalistic explanation–there is no need for wings when you are dealing with divine power. Or it may simply be that the image of angels that Ashley was acquainted with was a wingless one: "They looked like the stereotypical preconception of what an angel is supposed to look like, from the Western perspective. They were all very peaceful looking, very gentle, floating in the air [...]. No wings."

Just as popular culture in the form of Disney films likely influenced Ashley's perception of fairies, so a popular song may have provided Ashley with a particular expression for her angels. The expression "band of angels" does not come up in the Bible. Its most likely influence on Ashley comes from the first verse of the spiritual, "Swing Low, Sweet Chariot" by Harry T. Burleigh:

> Swing low, sweet chariot,
>
> Comin' fo' to carry me home!
>
> Swing low, sweet chariot,
>
> Comin fo' to carry me home.

I looked over Jordan, an' what did I see,

Comin fo' to carry me home?

A band of angels comin' after me,

Comin' fo' to carry me home!

It was Birke Duncan who found this correlation between Ashley's expression and the song.

The most notable contrast in the description between the fairies and the angels that Ashley reports may be that the angels have eyes–thus, there is an intimacy possible between Ashley and her angels which is impossible between her and the more alien fairies. She can look the angel in the eye–they are closer to her in their humanity, while the fairies represented to her a certain alien quality, with their blank faces. And, indeed, these angels appear to be praying at Ashley's bedside: clearly they are personally connected with Ashley, rather than more wayward visitors who pass by in the night. "I think with the fairies I was in the right place at the right time, because I didn't sense a message or anything like that. With the angels, I definitely sensed a feeling of peace, like things were going to be all right. There was a message there, even though it was unspoken." The psychological function of this memorate appears to be to bolster Ashley's faith and she makes clear that these angels did make her feel more secure, despite the anxieties regarding her father's absence. Ashley speaks of a feeling of "loss" in reaction to her father's departure, and the angels' influence counteracts this pain with "peace."

Ashley is willing to believe in both fairies and angels, though she is at the same time not naive. Like Sagan, she recognizes that belief comes at least partly from personal emotional needs: "Even if people aren't religious, they want to believe that there's something spiritual out there to take care of them. You see angels everywhere: in calendars, books, movies, TV shows, specials. People will be far more likely to believe the story about angels because they want to believe it." Ashley thus emphasizes the proliferation of the image of angels in our culture and the appeal on the gut level. Likewise, Carl Sagan offers his own impression that his parents have not actually died when he was not fully awakened in the morning as a testament to the tendency to believe in an afterlife despite empirical data: "Plainly there's something within me that's ready to believe in life after death. And it's not the least bit interested in whether there's any sober evidence for it...This is about humans being human" (203). Traditions of the supernatural speak to these psychological drives toward spiritual transcendence as well as revealing how the imagination mediates between one's inner world and the external environment, producing compelling narratives as a result which represent testaments of individual belief and cultural constructs that have historical depth.

Ashley's and Sean's accounts, however, are partly isolated from the matrix of tradition. They have not shared their stories with many other people or heard similar memorates– particularly as regards fairies. For both of them the media has played the role of unreliable tradition bearer, though their memorates achieve a certain independence from the influence of books, film and television. Ashley claims her fairies do not look like the fairies in the book, *Fairies*; and Sean denies that the film *Troll* had much bearing on his little people. While seemingly emancipated from the tyranny of folklore alterations by the media, the fact that it is the media alone which serves as a common reference point for Ashley and Sean emphasizes the lack of interpersonal communication of supernatural traditions in our modern world and the rather impersonal shadow of culture which lacks a human voice. The fact that we have collected mainly memorates (individual accounts of personal experience with the supernatural) rather than legends (tales that have been repeated enough that they are told as history within a particular community) indicates the tendency towards isolation rather than community—these tales are for the select few who might believe or least not mock, rather than a larger network who once upon a time would share in the anxieties and desires encoded in a story of an encounter with fairies.

Arthur Rackham, "Fairies Tiff with the Birds"

Chapter 4
"The River Boys"

by Bob McAllister
As told to an analyzed by Birke

Bainbridge High School teacher Bob McAllister told this tale to his fourth period English class from 12:57-2:00 on Thursday, October 29, 1998. He, the twenty teenagers, and I left their classroom and walked down a corridor to the stage. One classmate dimmed the lights. The students and I sat in a loose semi-circle on the floor, while Bob sat on a bench. My two tape recorders lay on the table next to him. The parenthetical (L) denotes laughter from the audience.

"The River Boys"

This story is not easy to tell. Some events in people's lives leave an indelible mark. There are times when things happen to us, when we look back upon them, we wonder, "Did this really happen?"

I tell this story, and some of you mentioned knowing from older people who have heard this. I tell it, every Halloween. And I'm serious that in some ways stories ward off evil. They become talismans, I think.

I think in some ways I've led a charmed life. Charmed because it hasn't been destroyed before now. And I'm not going to be destroyed this hour, this day. But whenever I'm in a room and I don't know if, or when, someone is coming, I turn around and I make sure I look. When I sit in a restaurant, I always have to face toward the largest part of the room. I want my back to something, where I can see most people. There's a reason for that.

On the other side, I think I have led a charmed life. I haven't ever told another class this, but when I was nine years old, I was riding my bicycle alone, for one of the first times. It was in Ballard, by Loyal Heights, where we lived. A car came behind me, about 35 or 40 miles per hour, heading straight for me, and I heard the car, and turned around, and suddenly my bike jerked to one side, threw me off, and the car sped by. This red haired woman came out and said, "You must have a guardian angel. I was looking at you, and suddenly your bike slammed off to the side about five feet. And if it hadn't, you would have been killed."

I didn't think too much of it at the time. Kids don't think about things too much.

But I've been telling this story ever since I was fourteen. The main events of it happened when I was twelve. It began a year before that, when I lived in Edmonds in Woodway Park. I think I've told you about the fact that my folks were very rich. My Dad had a sporting goods and bicycle store at First and Stewart [in Seattle], now a parking garage. He had a hardware store at 175th and Aurora. He owned Aurora Cycle, the big bicycle place by Greenlake. And he owned the first patent to those fishing pole holders, where you control them in a boat. You know, they screw onto the side of a boat, and you can put your pole in them and just leave it. They were manufacturing those just off of First and Stewart, in a part that was just above old Seattle.

I had three brothers, so there were four of us. Actually, I have four brothers, but one is way older. So there were four of us, basically, that were separated by about a year and a half. We used to visit that manufacturing place, and walk down the stairs. And you could look through these slats and see parts of old Seattle. You could see darkness. We'd pretend we could see rats, and kind of scare each other.

But life was as perfect as it could be. Every Christmas we got everything we wanted. My Dad would bring home samples from salesmen. You know: basketballs, slingshots. We built this giant basketball court right out in front of the house that was lit at night, so we could play basketball at night.

Every one of us loved baseball. That was the year, when I was eleven, that Little League baseball began. I don't mean across the United States; but it began up in Lynnwood, Edmonds, Alderwood Manor, Mountlake Terrace. So, of course, I tried out. For some reason, they must have parceled so many players per team, because I was playing for the Lynnwood Lions and all my friends were playing for the Edmonds Tigers. I played out the season with the Lynwood Lions, as did my brother Timmy, who later was scouted by the New York Yankees. And he was much better than I was. I wasn't bad, but he was really good. He could power that ball. He had a beautiful swing, if you know anything about baseball. Very smooth.

The next year, I was determined to play for the Edmonds Tigers, and I did. I pitched, played shortstop, and caught sometimes.

And so, my brother and I made the team. Practice started in the spring, and we were winning games. I had my blue baseball hat. It was a blue flannel hat, dark blue, with a gold E on it. And in those days, when you got a baseball hat, they weren't made of this synthetic stuff; they were flannel. And what you did was, you folded them up in a certain way. I could show you if I had a hat, but nobody wears those kinds of hats anymore. That's kind of disappearing. But we used to fold them up, crease the bill so it would look cool, then we'd put them under our bed

156

and sleep on them every night. That's what a baseball hat meant. It was part of you.

And putting on those beautiful uniforms for the first time; it was astounding. I was playing baseball with all my friends. I was happy. What would that have been, fifth grade, at the age of eleven? I think? Yeah. The season was going along.

And one day my Dad came home and told us we were moving to a place called North Ridge, Minnesota. It wasn't really in the north, so I don't know why they called it North Ridge. Maybe it had something to do with the ridge that was north of it. But it was mainly in the southern part of Minnesota. My Mom was born in Minneapolis, so he knew Minnesota a little bit. We were moving then. I mean, he was taking the whole family, because he was making so much money from fishing pole holders that he needed to start a factory back there. He was going to leave the business in the hands of my oldest brother, and then start up this factory.

North Ridge was a perfect place for a factory because it had a railroad spur coming in, and from there you could get to the Great Lakes, ship there, from there you could get to Chicago, and ship to points east and west. It was right in the center of where he could make a lot of money.

He said that we would be staying there for a year to two years, while he started it up. All of us complained. But of course, you can't say anything to your parents. I mean, that was it when you were young. I couldn't say [deep voice]: "No, I think I'll stay here and go to college" OR "No, I think I'll stay with my friends for the next couple of years."

So we had to move right after school got out, and I had to leave my baseball team with the last ten games, or something, left to be played. I was crushed. But, you keep on doing what you have to do.

And my Dad had gone back there about three weeks before, and had gotten a house for us to live in. He sent us back pictures. And he immediately had this sleeping pavilion built, because all of us boys loved to sleep out. We had sleepouts all the time. This sleeping pavilion had a roof over part of it; but the main part of it, right in the center, was open so you could sleep out at night under the stars. And if it started raining, you could get underneath the roof. It was probably about the size of this stage. I would bet. Yeah, about sixteen by twenty-four [feet] or so.

We were pretty excited about that. And I know now that he did it so we could feel better about moving to North Ridge, and not having any friends.

So, we moved back. I played with my brothers for the first couple days. And we'd play pickle. You know that baseball game where the person runs the bases, and you throw the ball, and try to get them in a pickle. And we'd do that.

We lived on Wachusetts Road. And by the third day, it gets pretty old, just having your brothers to play with. I hadn't met anyone. I was walking down to get the mail, and heard these footsteps. They weren't footsteps;

159

they were pounding steps behind me. My baseball hat was taken off my head. And here was this guy, about my age, running down the road. So I ran after him, grabbed him, and got my hat back. He said, "Hi, my name is Lee Grant. What's yours?"

And I said, "Bob McAllister."

He said, "Did you just move here?"

I said, "Yeah."

He said, "Well, come on over to my house."

I said, "Okay, let's go over to my house. You can meet my Mom, and then I can go over to your house."

And so we went over to his house. Lee had two sisters, one named Carol, and one named Miriam. Carol was older, and you'll see her later on in the story. Miriam died about fourteen years after I met Lee. She committed suicide. I liked her.

They had a horse, a roan. Isn't that a roan, kind of speckled? Not speckled. It was patches of orange and white. Is that a roan?

[Girl: It's a pinto.]

Oh, pinto. There you go. Pinto! Pinto! And Carol had named the horse Beauty. Lee and I would ride it sometimes. I wasn't much of a rider, but he would ride it. They had a big barn out there that we could play in.

He quickly introduced me to two kids down there: John Delano & John Bjornson, who lived down the road a ways. And the four of us started to get together. And so, the next day, we met.

My Dad had told me: "I don't care where you play around here, but I don't want you to go down by the railroad tracks. There's rumors that bad people hang out there."

Of course, that was the first place I wanted to go. I don't know if you know how it is, when you move to a new place, kids that live there want to show you the places that are significant, immediately; especially if they are a little bit forbidden.

We went down to the railroad tracks where there was a rumored shantytown. It was probably an old Hooverville. There was just a bunch of junk around, and some tin, and a couple of garbage cans. That wasn't too exciting.

Maybe I wasn't too impressed because Lee said, "Okay, if you want to see something really scary…"

Right up from the railroad tracks, you could climb this hill. The closest thing I can think of is those hills above Fay-Bainbridge State Park; those clay banks that you climb up, a steep climb. We climbed up those. When we got to the top, they said they were gonna take me to the haunted house.

Every place has a haunted house. The one on Bainbridge Island used to be just down this road, where Ordway [Elementary School] is now, right as the hill starts to go on. It was rumored there was a woman who killed her husband there. It had broken windows, and looked like that house in Psycho, kind of Victorian and old.

This house that they took me to, which they called "The Haunted House of North Ridge", sat in the middle of this meadow as you got up on top of the cliff. Here was this two story house, with this covered porch around it, all

162

rotted, falling down. And of course, we went during the day. But we got in the front door, which was hanging off its hinges. We looked around. There was a bunch of graffiti on the walls, some old beer bottles, and an old mattress in the living room. And there was a kitchen with no sink in it. Everything smelled musty. It was interesting. They told me some old story about–heh–this psychopathic killer had been there, murdered seven people, or something like that. And that was kind of cool. I was impressed.

On our way home, they took me past this Scandinavian cemetery. Cemeteries are always neat to walk through because there are dead people under the ground (L). I used to imagine that, as we were walking. And that's why you never walk directly on a grave because you don't want to wake up somebody down below.

But right in the middle was this domed building. You could actually go inside. It was a mausoleum. And when you walked inside, if you looked to the left, there were four stones; and to the right, four stones; and straight ahead were six or eight. And they all contained the names of Scandinavian people. And I still remember there was a Sandvik: S-A-N-D-V-I-K. I still have a photographic memory for spelling. And there was a Thorsen: T-H-O-R-S-E-N. They were all dated way back. Scandinavian settlers came there in the eighteen-hundreds. The dates were 1812-1880. And there was no one in there, this mausoleum, that hadn't died after 1890. That was pretty exciting.

And we four quickly became great friends. Of course, if you have four kids, you start to have a club, at least when you're twelve years old. We thought, "Okay, we'll have a club."

We decided to call ourselves…It was actually my name. I had been reading *Huck Finn* and *Tom Sawyer*, and I was in love with the idea of going down the Mississippi, so I said, "Why don't we call ourselves The River Boys?"

It's strange, because there was no river anywhere nearby, but we called ourselves The River Boys.

John Delano, who had something of an artistic bent, made up little cards that said, "The River Boys." And it had a kind of river running through it, and then it had an X down where we signed our names. And we kept those cards in our wallets. I could show you the card, except I don't have it anymore. I have no idea where it went. It must have been lost; or maybe I put it away because I didn't want to see it. Or maybe I didn't want to be reminded about it. But you can't ever really forget anything. You have to remember. I have to remember everything, and especially things that [sigh] that went the way The River Boys went.

We had a special language. It sounds stupid now, but when we didn't like someone, we called them a wane: W-A-N-E. If you were ever anywhere, and one of us said, "Bedeebedud" it was a signal that we should make excuses and get out of there. We started sleeping over, especially at my house. Since I had three other brothers, we had to make a reservation, so I'd make one for The River Boys. It was not so much of a problem in the summer.

In the summer, we would do things. We would sneak out, of course, which was one of the great benefits of sleeping out late at night. And we'd sleep out, and then sneak out around ten or eleven, we'd go over to Grant's house, and grab some hay. We'd each grab a giant handful. There was a road about fifty feet away. And we'd put a big mound of hay right around this corner. And I don't advise you guys doing this (L). Big mound of hay, right around a corner, so a car would come around the corner and have to slam on his brakes (L). It was cool to sit there in the darkness and watch this. Completely illegal, of course, but it was fun (L).

This never worked: we did the dog manure in the sack, lighting it on fire, putting in the porch trick. Every time, someone would open the door, look at this flaming sack, go in, get some water to throw on it, and yell, "What the hell are you kids doing?" (L)

I think we tried that twice.

And then we go to the one where we'd stand out in the middle of the road that was about a half mile away.

Then we'd see headlights coming toward us. The idea was to stand there, the four of us, and the last one to leave was the most brave. It usually ended up being Grant. Usually, I was second or third. Bjornson was usually the first to take off (L). But that was exciting.

I also used to play the hunchback of Notre Dame. I'd stick a pillow in my back, and then Grant and Delano would get a rope and put it around my neck, and I'd go out in front of cars as the hunchback (L). And sometimes they'd beat me with a stick when cars went by to see if they'd stop. Nobody ever stopped.

I think the best one that summer was a game where I think Grant came up with it. If you can imagine this, there was this curvy road, and a big bank up above it, and then telephone poles up here. Grant got an old purse, patent leather, and I got some make-up stuff from my Mom. Delano or Bjornson got some handkerchiefs and an old pack of cigarettes that had a couple cigarettes in it. What we did was this: tie fishing line around the handle, up on top of the hill, we threw the purse over the telephone wire

167

so it landed down in the road. Then we arranged all the stuff so it looked like someone had dropped the purse.

It worked. EVERY TIME, IT WORKED! The first car came by, stopped, and went on past it–which was cool– stopped the car, and came back. I think it was a woman the first time. She bent down to pick it up, we jerked on the wire, the purse went flying up in the air, and she [haggish scream:]: AAAH!" (L) Ha, ha!

That was fun! We did it again. It was very dangerous. Sometimes people would stop on the curve, then go down to pick up the purse. We got pretty good at it. Sometimes they'd come to get the purse and we'd jerk it just a little bit. They'd reach down to pick it up, and then they'd wonder whether it really moved or not. It was like there was something alive in there. Ha, ha! (L).

By this time, we were really good at it, very subtle. The purse was down there and this car stopped. A guy got out and went to get the purse. We were all watching him, and just enjoying manipulating other people. We gave it a little jerk and immediately–I don't know whether he'd played this thing or not–but he immediately looked up the bank to where we were, right into four pairs of eyes, and started running up the bank like he was going downhill. I mean that guy must have been a Marine or some kind of athlete, because he was booking up that hill (L). He was halfway up before we realized what was happening. We just ditched in the woods and never came back there. We were afraid of that guy; never wanted to meet him again.

So, the school year started. We were all in the sixth grade. And in the sixth grade, you had recess. We always played flag football. You guys know flag football? And it kind of got out. The River Boys was an exclusive club. We had it going for two months, so we didn't want anyone else in it. But it quickly got out. I always played quarterback on my team, because I was a good passer. Bjornson was a pretty tall kid. If he and I were together, we always won because he would catch my passes. He was taller than any kid in the sixth grade. So he'd say, "That's one for The River Boys! The River Boys win again."

That's how it got out that we had this club. Well, there was this kid named Marvin Gorsuch: G-O-R-S-U-C-H. And Marvin had very thick glasses, and hair that never seemed combed. It kind of stuck up in thatches. He was the kind of kid that nobody talked to. He was kind of like Leper [Lepellier from *A Separate Peace* by John Knowles]. He was that kind of kid. I don't recall him ever even saying a word in class, or outside of it. He came up to us, as we were coming in from recess, one day probably around the first of October, when school had been going on for four, five, or six weeks. Marvin said [haltingly], "Uh, I want to join your club."

We looked at him [head tilted], because he'd never said anything to us before. I don't think he ever talked to anyone in class. He was just alone. And someone said, "You wanna join The River Boys?"

And he said, "Yeah. What do you have to do?"

So Delano said, "Well, it's...We only do initiations once a year on Halloween. And what you do is you have to sleep over at McAllister's and, you get up at twelve-midnight, and have to go by yourself to the Scandinavian churchyard, and collect a note that we'll put inside the tomb that says, 'River Boys.' Then you have to go to the haunted house above the railroad tracks and collect another note. And when you get back, you pass the initiation, and you become a River Boy."

I was listening to this and thinking, "God, I don't remember ever talking about an initiation." (L) Then I realized, "Oh, he made that up just then."

I really admired him for it. I never could have come up with something like that, cool and complicated, because it was the way to keep Marvin from joining the club.

About a week later, my Mom, who was President of the Methodist Church Women's Auxiliary, or something like that, said when I got home: "Oh, Bobby, Mrs. Gorsuch called."

I had already reserved the sleeping porch for The River Boys for Halloween. I love Halloween.

My Mom said Mrs. Gorsuch had called and said that Marvin was sleeping over with The River Boys. I said, "No. No, Mom. Marvin isn't sleeping over. He's not one of The River Boys."

She said, "Well, Mrs. Gorsuch said that he was invited."

And I said, "Oh…"

I couldn't tell my Mom all of the details, because some part of me knew it wasn't right. But also my Mom was a friend of Mrs. Gorsuch's, so I couldn't refuse to have her come. I don't know if you've been in a bind like that, but I couldn't say no.

So Halloween came and I think it was on a Saturday. In fact, it had to be on Saturday, because we all met in the morning. I swiped a couple of those Mason canning jars from my Mom. Delano made a couple of the notes that said, "The River Boys" and put them in the jars. We didn't think Marvin would come, but we were sure that he wouldn't be able to go out at midnight, on

172

Halloween night, and go out to the graveyard, and go to the haunted house.

So we put the notes there. Plus we wanted to scare ourselves, too, maybe. It was a lot easier in broad daylight, of course, with three other guys with you. We went and we put one note in the mausoleum under Sandvik. The stones were about like this: [holding his hands straight, sideways, one over the other] so a body could be put in this way. It was about five inches, so we could just fit the canning jar underneath the stone. We put it all the way to the left, which we figure was the darkest place, and most terrible. We were scaring ourselves, at that point, more than we wanted to scare Marvin. I don't know if that makes any sense, but we were imagining what it would be like if he did.

We went out to the haunted house, and we put the second underneath what was the kitchen sink, in the cupboard, shoved in the back among the collapsing, rotten wood.

Halloween night came, and sure enough, Marvin came, both Johns, and Lee.

I think I felt closer to Lee than any of the other guys because of stuff that happened later. I loved Lee, at that time. I think I'd love him now if he were still alive. I wish I could see him. I wish his life hadn't turned out the way it did. But that's ahead, in the future.

So Marvin came over. His Mom drove him. We were in the sixth grade, so we just wore masks. We didn't do a big deal about dressing up. We went out and did all the trick-or-treating stuff, but when we got enough, we started ringing doorbells, running off, and hiding. Ringing doorbells! That's so much fun!

Then we came home and my mother made us cocoa and toast. If you've never had cocoa and toast, try it sometime. It's so good, and it was such a treat. It got to be about ten o'clock, so I stowed away some of my candy because I didn't want those guys eating it. I wanted to save it, for the next week.

We went out into the sleeping pavilion. What we liked at that time was, of course, candy. We brought a bunch of candy with us. And we brought those God-awful Nehi soft drinks that were in glass at that time. They had this brilliant orange-colored drink, this sickening green concoction, and a purple drink; all these wild colors. And we also liked hotdogs, without cooking them.

[Girl: That's gross.]

I know. And we also liked Lik-M-Aid [Fun Dip]; this stuff that's pure sugar. You open up the package and then you lick it.

[Girl: I've had some of that stuff.]

Yeah! So cool! We sat there and we ate.

And we told the story about, what is it, about those two kids that are out parking and there's a psychopathic killer loose, who's got a silver claw. They go out there and park. I think it was a story, at the time, meant to get kids to stop parking–quote: "watching the submarine races." It's like, "You're not really there watching submarine

175

races, because you can't see them." You're just being with your girl, or your guy.

The story of "The Hook" is always very scary. These two kids are out there, and they hear over the radio that a psychopathic killer called The Hook has escaped from a mental hospital and everybody's alerted. And they're out there in this God-forbidden stretch of strange forest, where they're all alone in the dark.

She says, "Let's get out of here. I don't want to take chances with The Hook."

And he says, "No, let's stay here, honey. We'll be fine."

She says, "No! We should get going."

And so he gets angry. He starts the car and, you know, jams out of there.

And when they get back to her home to drop her off, he gets out of the car and goes around to the side. There is a silver hook, with nothing on it, grabbed around the door.

SCARY! Very scary. Well, it seemed scary at the time.

Then we told another story about the Peg-Legged Ghost, or something like that. It turns out the Peg-Legged Ghost kills young kids. You know, we told that stuff and tried to scare each other.

Marvin just sat there listening. He never said a word. Ever. Nothing. It was like, we four were such good friends, we ignored him. I have to say it. We ignored him, which wasn't right, but it was the self-involvement of being twelve.

So it came twelve-midnight, and we counted down to it because we were expecting something momentous to happen. Twelve-midnight came, and we said, "Marvin, time to go" -never thinking that he would.

He stood up and grabbed one of our flashlights and said, "I'll see you later, I think."

He went off through the woods. We didn't say a word. We watched him as he went off. We saw the flashlight go through the path, headed toward the cemetery. I think someone, after a while, said, "Wow. He's really gonna go."

We kind of just accepted it, the way a twelve-year-old accepts anything that happens; and didn't think too much about it. The crummy thing was we figured if he was moving fast, maybe he'd get back by twelve-thirty. He would be moving fast on a night like that because it was the kind of night with a full moon, nicely enough, and clouds moving across it. So every once in a while, you'd have the full light, and then the darkness in the shape of the clouds.

We decided what we'd do is stuff our sleeping bags and go outside the sleeping pavilion, then when he came back, jump out and scare him.

So we stuffed our sleeping bags at about twelve-twenty or something like that. We went out, each of us in a different part. And that's when it got a little bit scary for me, even though the other guys were there. There was a wind moving through the branches; there was a full moon;

there was nobody else around; there were sounds in the forest. We all had our Boy Scout watches, at that time.

They only had them out on the market for maybe two years max because you would press something here, and then the dial would light up. What they found was, it had a little radioactive implant. Every time you pressed it, you were giving yourself a little dose of radiation (L). I didn't know it at the time, but that's true. That's what was happening.

So we stayed out there. Twelve-thirty came: no Marvin. Twelve-thirty-five: no Marvin. Twelve-forty: still no Marvin. Finally one of us–I can't remember who–said, "Maybe we'd better talk."

We all went back to the pavilion, which wasn't far away. It was only like from here to, I don't know, halfway to the light booth.

So we all went back. We didn't know what to do. At that time, there was a great fear that someone would sprain their ankle. Every kid was afraid of spraining their ankle, for some reason It was the equivalent of a fatal

179

disease. We thought maybe Marvin had sprained his ankle, and he was having trouble getting back. We weren't bad kids. We were not bad kids. We didn't want to hurt Marvin. That was one thing that could have happened. The other thing that could have happened was maybe he'd just gone home. Maybe he saw through what we were doing to him, and he went home, in which case I would have been in a lot of trouble. So we determined that the only thing we could do, at that point, was to re-track his steps and see if indeed he had gone out to the cemetery.

So we took off, the four of us, and went down the trail and out onto the road, and then into the cemetery. And that's scary regardless of whether you've got three people with you or– well, probably three hundred might be okay. Four of us walking across those cemetery stones over to the mausoleum and opening up the door, and only the flashlight, and then shining that light over to where Sandvik's burial site was. And I can still see the flashlight shining as Delano picked up the Mason Jar and held it up to the light. And there was no note inside of it. The interesting thing was the lid. It was as if someone had been very careful, because the lid was put back the same way it had been. It was in the same spot where we had put it that day. We knew he had gotten that far.

Then we went to, of course, the house on the hill, and walked up to that field. You know that almost wheat-like stuff that grows up around this high [three feet] and it has little seeds on the end? If you take them–it's an old trick–you take the seeds and say, "Here, I have a trick for you." You put them in someone's mouth, halfway, and then you pull it, and it makes them have seeds in their mouth. Have you ever done that? (L) [Nasalized:] It's really a cool trick. You should try it sometime (L).

It was a field like that. All this wheat–or whatever it was–was blowing. Shapes of the clouds were moving across. And the wind was blowing. We looked up toward this dark house on the hill.

We went upon the porch, with one flashlight for all four of us. I was either second or third. I never wanted to be first because the monster could always get you from the front, of course. And you never wanted to be in the back because someone would grab the person from the back and eliminate them one-by-one. So I was always right in the middle. We went into the kitchen and shined that light to where the jar was, and the note was still in the jar.

And we were looking at that, right at that point, we heard this sound. I've never heard a sound like it after, ever, in my life. It was both liquid and, it was something breaking. But it wasn't like snapping. It was absolutely right up on the second story. We knew the direction from which it came. We didn't talk, but we had to go. We had to head to where that noise was.

And so we walked up the stairs and, as you'd walk down the hallway, there was a door on your left, and a door straight ahead, and a door on the right. And the door on the right was open. And there was the moon coming in. So there was light. I think we all knew that that was the room. We didn't talk. None of us could talk by that time. We were just moving. I think Delano was in front, and I was second. In fact, I know I was second, but I think it was

Delano. It could have been Bjornson. I came up behind Delano and he stopped at the door, with the flashlight. He was frozen. I came up over his shoulder, to look in, and there was Marvin in the corner of the room.

But the way his head was...He was slumped down in the corner. He was...I don't know if you would call it sitting, but he was in a corner of the room. His head was bent in a way that no living person's can be; the way his head was on him. It was on, but he was dead.

[A blonde girl, six feet to Bob's right, had looked away; but then she looked straight at him.]

And we of course–I don't know if this is of course– we ran. I've never run so fast. I can't remember if we screamed, if we yelled, but it was a sense of everybody bounding down the stairs, and then running home, all the way. By that time we knew we had to tell my folks first.

So I woke up my Mom and Dad. They made sure we were telling the truth, then called the police; and called up the other parents. The police came over at some point. Time gets really weird and screwy. They took us each into separate rooms and asked us. I can remember Mrs. Gorsuch coming by. I can remember my little brother, Lee, coming down the stairs in his cowboy and Indian pajamas, and rubbing his eyes, not knowing what was going on.

The preacher came over the next day, and talked to me for a while. We all got sent to a psychiatrist in town that next week.

They investigated, of course. They think that probably what happened was when Marvin went up there, he probably surprised someone. They put it on a transient, as they always do. They blame the poor people or the people they don't know. They never found him. Marvin had had his neck broken by a good deal of force. It takes force to break a human neck.

My folks were very good. They moved us out of there very fast, within two weeks, we'd moved back into the Edmonds area; different house this time. Lee Grant moved there in about six months. His folks and my folks were good friends.

And I just kind of, I put it away. You know? Well, Suse [from *Rumors of Peace* by Ella Leffland] talks about different compartments in the brain where you can put things away. And sometime, when I was about fourteen, about two years later, I started telling that story at night, when we'd have sleepouts. I had sleepouts until I was sixteen. I stopped because it was more fun to drive a car with a girl than it was to sleep out with the guys. I started to tell that story, and it got to be a very big deal. People would say, "Oh, let's invite McAllister. He can tell that story."

But I told it like it wasn't true, because I could believe it wasn't true. I don't know if that makes any sense, but that's why I did it.

Lee Grant and I had a history together. We did a lot of things first, together. We double-dated. We bought our first motorcycles together, and then he took off for San Francisco when he was about nineteen, with about a thousand bucks of mine that I'd loaned him. He was wanted by the police for writing bad checks. But, you know, some guys go through that.

I went to the University of Washington. In my junior year, I had hardly any money at all. I'd go over to my Mom's. This was about ten/eleven years after it happened. I would go over to my Mom's for dinner, because she made great dinners. I would stock up on food. Plus my Dad– no, my Dad was still around, so it had to be after that. Okay, it had to be a year after that, when I was a senior. I went over there one night for a nice, big dinner. And she told me she'd gotten a letter from Mrs. Delano back in North Ridge.

And John had stayed there. He was a hometown boy. They'd built a reservoir in that place, in North Ridge, outside of it, and they'd stocked it with fish. John had been found dead. They'd sent along a clipping. He had gone fishing by himself in the early morning, and they found him face up in the boat. Cause of death was some kind of congenital heart thing that nobody had ever spotted. I thought about John, because he was a very important part of my life, at one time, and now he was gone. I didn't make a connection. I thought about The River Boys, of course, but I didn't make much of a connection.

And then, I started teaching. I came to Bainbridge Island. Some time after that, I was in Seattle on a Saturday, and I saw this article in the *Seattle Times*. In fact, I was reading it on the ferry on the way over. It was an article about: "Father killed by son." It was John Bjornson of Arlington, Washington, who was out hunting with his son. He was thirty-five, something like that. My age. John Bjornson, spelled the same, hunting with his son. They'd gone through a fence, and his son's gun had tripped and shot him, taking, as I found out later, about half his head off. The son was twelve, I think, something like that.

My Mom was gone by then. I couldn't talk to her. I called up and asked the Arlington coroner for John Bjornson's place of birth, because I thought I might know him. It was North Ridge, Minnesota, which gave me pause to think. Now two out of those four people were gone.

And once I found out about that, I started wondering about Lee Grant, because I hadn't seen him in twenty years. I called up Pete Maier, who was a US District Attorney at the time, and said, "Can you track Lee Grant for me?"

Pete had connections to the FBI. I figured Grant would have a criminal record, because he already had one at twenty. [Pete] got back to me in two days and he said Lee was in prison in Oregon.

Lee was part of the cocaine distribution from California, through the State of Oregon to Washington. And he was serving five-to-ten, and he'd already served four years, but he was still alive. So I wrote him a letter, and didn't think much about it. He never answered. Grant wasn't the kind to answer letters.

Very charming guy; very charismatic kind of guy. If you saw him today in high school, girls would just follow him around because he was a good looking guy. Had a lot of charm. He was also a manipulator, absolutely, but he had a lot of charm.

One of my friends, Steve Johnson, got a letter from Grant saying that he was out of prison, and he was coming up this summer. It was the summer of '86. I was going through some rough times then, and I wanted to see Lee Grant because he and I did so much together. And I kept on waiting for him. It's not like I was waiting for him, but I had, in the back of my head: "Good deal. I get to see Lee." I wanted to see what he was like after thirty years, or whatever it was, that I hadn't seen him.

It was one August night, about the middle of August, and suddenly it hit me: "I haven't seen Lee."

I was by myself, and I was feeling down. I go through periods when I feel depressed. I haven't told you that but I do at times. I wanted to talk to Lee. I wanted to make a connection. It was kind of late at night.

I knew that Carol Grant, his sister, worked down at VIPS, down in Renton. I called up, and Carol was there. I said, "I heard that Lee was coming up this summer. When is he coming?"

She said, "My God, you haven't heard."

I said, "No. What happened?

She said, "I'll call you back."

She called me back in ten minutes, when she could get to a private phone, because she was a bartender. She said that Lee had gotten out of prison and, probably about a month before I called, he had died.

What happened was he had come back and immediately started the Northern California marijuana growers' association. Fairly illegal. But that's how he was making his money. Living with a woman, who was supporting him, and he had this marijuana field up in the California mountains. And he had this four-wheel-drive vehicle, to get to it.

Now I think it might be a drug-related killing. I don't think this was an accident. At first, I thought, "Oh, a complete accident." What they found in his car was an empty pint bottle of Tequila. And as I think back on it, when he was seventeen, if I would have had the education you guys have, I would have known: "Boy, here is a guy heading toward alcoholism." He always drank real heavy.

But they found this empty bottle he would have picked up at the liquor store, because there was a receipt for it, which was maybe fifteen minutes away. He'd killed a whole pint of Tequila between the picking up of the bottle, and him getting to the field. When he got to the field, he parked on the wrong side of the road, for who knows why, and got (at least the way the police said and the way Carol said) he got out on the wrong side and went straight down about a hundred and fifty feet, down to the bottom of this cliff, and probably broke nearly every bone in his body.

As they retraced it, sometime during the night–because Lee was always good with camping out–he built some kind of shelter over himself, because it gets cold there at night. Then the next day, he had dragged himself over to the stream, being dehydrated with the injury and the alcohol. That's where they found him three days later, with his head in the stream. They figured that he probably put his head in to get a drink of water and couldn't get it back out again because, no strength.

I heard that late at night, and I said, "Thanks for telling me, Carol" and hung up. And boy, everything came back about all those guys who were in The River Boys, and I was the last one.

And then I started thinking, "Good God, what's going to happen now?"

That's when I started telling the story again. I think about that cycle because it doesn't happen immediately. All of those deaths were spaced out. I think that my turn came, and it didn't happen.

There was a boy who went to school here, who I taught from the time he was in the ninth grade. He was a very inner boy. He was in a theater class, when he was a senior. Sometime during the spring, I started to get calls on the phone where this low, disguised voice would say, "I want to talk to Satan."

And I can't hear Satan without laughing. Heh. At first, I couldn't hear him. I said, "Yes, this is Satan. This is six-six-six." (L)

And then: no answer. I just waited and then: click.

192

And I got another call. And again it said, "I want to talk to Satan."

I said, "Well, this is Satin, not Satan. You got the spelling wrong." (L)

Because of that "Mr. Fritts is Satin"--that misspell; that great graffiti on the desk.

I didn't think much about it. Then...I can't remember when this is, but not too long ago, I think I avoided the whole thing. What happened was this: this kid had gotten the idea that I was the Antichrist. I mean, he had this delusion. I'm not really the Antichrist (L). And he was the son of Moses, who had been chosen to kill me.

His plan was; at the Moving Up assembly–you guys know that–during a time when various announcements were being made, he was going to take me to the front, and slash my throat. You can do that very quickly by hitting the carotid, right there [running his finger down the left side of his neck]. And you're dead real fast.

Of course, it was a great idea. It was a wonderful idea because everyone would think: "Oh, theater." He was going to do it right as I presented the theater awards. It was brilliant. Everybody would have thought: "God, funny! That's acting."

[Girl: And you would be dead?]

Pardon?

[Girl: Would you be dead?]

And then I would be dead.

As it happened: the day came, the assembly came, and Mr. Fritts [the Vice Principal] came over and said, "Now you can't take ten minutes like you took last year. You've got to be done in five."

I got upset, because I want those awards to last what they last. I said, "Well, I tell you, I'll just not do it. I'm not gonna do it if I can't take all the time."

He said, "Okay, we'll scratch you off the program."

I said, "Fine." Heh, heh (L).

I thought, "Okay, to hell with it." I was the last on the awards list, so I was canceled off it.

Then another teacher came over. It might have been Miss Sullivan, who said, "Will you pass out flowers to the seniors?"

I said [suave smile and tilted eyebrows]: "Sure."

Right at this point, I ducked underneath the grand-stands. And I'd been standing over in the little lobby area, where the seniors usually sit. I ducked underneath. Right at this point was when this guy was looking for me, and I disappeared. Plus I was on the schedule to be a speaker, but I wasn't.

As I got around to the other side, I see this kid coming out with a female teacher; and he's got her by the arm, and dragging her over to the microphone, and shouting. I looked and I thought, "God! Good for him. He's doing a theater thing. He's really learned."

And what was funny was Matt Hadlock, the kid who was running sound. [The assassin] was yelling something, but nobody could hear him because something was screwed up with the mike. Matt was madly trying to fix the microphone so he could be heard.

Then the next thing we saw was this kid, this senior–Dave Prout who used to work at the vid store—grabbed [the assassin] by one side, and then you saw the knife [the assassin] had in his hand. Then Mr. Ellick [the principal] went over and grabbed him, because he saw what was going on. Then [the assassin] is being carried out by Bim Prince & Jim Dow. And he's yelling, as he gets out the door: "You'll remember me for this!"

I was stunned.

I went back to the office and, of course, the talk was buzzing. Georgia [Figgins, the school secretary] told me that someone said that [the assassin] thought McAllister was the Antichrist. A teacher who was listening to this said, "Yeah, so what else is new?" Heh, heh, heh! (L)

It was funny, I thought, in the circumstances.

[The assassin] was under care of a psychiatrist. He's not around here anymore. I'm under witness protection.

But I start to think, "Maybe that was the confluence of events, and my time."

I also think about that sound we heard, and that was probably when Marvin got his neck snapped. I also think about opening that door, and maybe the guy was right behind it. Maybe that's why the door was partially open. Maybe he was waiting there.

[A theater door opened, letting in some sunlight, but no one entered.]

Whenever someone comes...

[The students shuddered and giggled nervously.]

Whenever anybody comes in a door like that, I always watch, because I'm not sure even now if sometimes the things we do...Absolutely, I was responsible for Marvin. And now, every one of us is gone. And right around Halloween is always the time when I begin to think maybe something is gonna come back.

Maybe something is gonna fall out of the sky. Maybe...
AAAH!

[Bob clutched at his throat. His eyes bugged out, he gasped, hissed, choked, shrieked and collapsed.] (L)

[Applause]

I hope you have a pleasant Halloween. If I'm not here Monday, you'll know why.

[It was the end of the school day, so most of the students left to catch buses, walk home, or head off to some activity. Several lingered afterward.]

Girl #1: That's what you said last year.

Bob: I did?

Girl #1: Yeah: "If I'm not here on Monday, you'll know why." That really freaked me out.

Bob: It did?

Girl #1: I was like: "Oh, my God, how could he say that?"

Ben: My Dad was a Loyal Heights student.

Bob: How old is your Dad?

Ben: He's [unintelligible].

Bob: Oh, okay. Wow. Gosh, yeah. I used to live on Cyrus.

Ben: I was born in Edmonds.

Bob: You were born where?

Ben: Edmonds.

Bob: You were? God, Ben.

Ben: Coincidence.

Bob: Yeah, Loyal Heights Elementary. I went there. Did you go there? Oh, that's closed down by that time. But your Dad went to Loyal Heights. I wonder if some of those old teachers were there. Mrs. Peacock.

Ben: I should have him come and talk to you sometime.

Bob: Yeah, I'd love it.

Girl #2: How did you know that noise came from the snapping of his neck?

Bob: How was it?

Girl #2: Yeah.

Bob: You know how you snap something hard, like a stick, or a bone, if you've ever snapped that. I think that it was liquid because of the cartilage and so on. And I've never heard anything like that sound since. Maybe if I was a hunter I would, if I went out and wrestled live bears or something. But, yeah.

Lynn: My sister still remembers, since she was coming to school late, the day of the assembly.

Bob: Oh…?

Lynn: My Mom was driving her, and there was this whole big, huge thing, like police cars and all this stuff. She got there when they were already coming.

Bob: Oh, after.

Lynn: She was like, "What's going on?" I can't remember why she was late.

Bob: That's another incident where you think, "Boy did that really happen?" It's very strange. I hope the kid is okay. But if he ever comes back, in the next four years, then the police will notify me. [Mocking nasalization:] Witness protection (L).

Lynn: It's scary.

Bob: Good-bye.

Lynn: Bye. Thank you.

Bob: Thank you, Lynn.

***

This marked the real end of the performance. By then, different students had arrived to work on stage construction for the upcoming play, *Is There a Comic in the House?*

Analysis

Analysis of "The River Boys" is no simple task. This complicated story requires me to divide my examination into separate parts, in order to examine one facet at a time. We will start with relevant biographical information about the raconteur, move on to applications of folk narrative, the supernatural subtext, connections to tradition, the ironic use of pranks; and look at some effects of crime on this story and verbal lore in general.

Biographical Information

Robert Charles McAllister was born on March 16, 1941, in Seattle, and raised in Edmonds. He earned a degree in English from the University of Washington and instructed drama, composition, speech, and literature from 1965 to 2014. Bob maintained a parallel career as a carpenter, during vacation time away from education. He taught for two years at Wenatchee High School, and transferred to Bainbridge High School, Bainbridge Island, Washington in 1967. Bob later chaired the English Department, and directed many popular school plays.

Some participants went on to entertainment careers. A few examples include Dove Cameron, Emmy winning star of *Liv and Maddie*, Tony and Obie winning costume and set designer David Zinn, and comedian Chris Kattan. The latter said in his autobiography that Bob had to discipline him for unruly silliness during rehearsals of *The Crucible*.

Bob retired from teaching at Bainbridge High School, then taught speech and composition for Olympic College in Bremerton and Poulsbo.

Bainbridge Island has a strong amateur theater tradition, dating back to a nineteenth century production of *HMS Pinafore*. Bob appeared in numerous community plays for Bainbridge Performing Arts (BPA), Island Theater (IT), and Ovation. He also dabbled in professional stage roles. The first was Jonathan Brewster, the villain, in a Seattle production of *Arsenic & Old Lace* in 1988. Bob's best reviewed work was in a 1991 stage version of *Willy Wonka & the Chocolate Factory*, which ran for four months at the Pioneer Square Theater in downtown Seattle. He portrayed Grandpa Joe, an exuberant ninety-year-old hypochondriac. Other parts have included Merlin in *Dance the Dragon Home*, an original open-air play at the Bloedel Reserve on Bainbridge Island; the villain in a virtually unpublicized family musical, *Saving Father Christmas,* and as Prof. Henry Higgins in a Port Angeles Light Opera production of *My Fair Lady.*

Bob also acted on camera. He portrayed a punk rock bass player, among other parts, in a 1989 music video for a late night local TV show, *Bombshelter Videos*; plus the lead dramatic role in *Lift Your Burdens Up*, a European MTV video for the rock band The Walkabouts, directed by Garrett Bennett. Bob also had cameos in two of Mr. Bennett's features, *Farewell to Harry* and *A Relative Thing*. Independent filmmaker Garrett L. Bennett was also one of Bob's students.

Applied Folklore

Theatrical experience has some bearing on storytelling. Differences abound between drama and oral narratives, but both require performance in front of a group and immersion in a story. "The River Boys" is also a solo play along the lines of *Give 'Em Hell, Harry* starring James Whitmore, *The Belle of Amherst* starring Julie Harris, and *Mark Twain Tonight!* Starring Hal Holbrook. Bob had the longplay vinyl record album of the latter performance, in his classroom.

I asked him if he had based the title "The River Boys" on Edward Stratemeyer's juvenile late nineteenth and early twentieth century book series about "The Rover Boys." Definitely not. The title was, as Bob says in the story, influenced by Huckleberry Finn and Tom Sawyer's adventures on the Mississippi River.

Bob's performance also ties in to a memory theory set forth by a Finnish scholar, Pirjo Korkiakangas, regarding nostalgia:

"Telling of childhood begins to observe the rules of drama. The narrator tries to develop the plot [...] and [...] events are woven into a thematic entity. The basic theme [...] may be expanded into a broader interpretation of childhood, the main support of which is nostalgia" (67).

Mr. McAllister knows "the rules of drama" intimately, and how to apply them, without over-indulgence in nostalgia.

Bob insists on context-dependence for any tale related in class, so that the activity does not turn into an "ego journey." The raconteur has a voluminous repertoire of oral narratives, but has described "The River Boys" as his piece-de-resistance. His personal experience stories are a way to model creative writing assignments, or to illustrate a theme from a reading assignment.

The ritual pops up in "The River Boys" when the narrator compares his assassin to Leper Lepellier from *A*

Separate Peace by John Knowles. Leper is a psychotic outsider in the novel. This reference provides a common association between listener and audience, and reminds them that they are still part of a literature class. "The River Boys" remains a festive activity, but Bob finds a way to connect it to course work.

I first heard a short version of "The River Boys" around Halloween of 1984, in a literature class. A couple of students pulled down the shades and turned out the lights. Some of us stayed at our desks, but at least half of the thirty teens huddled on the carpet, at Bob's feet. Even then the story ended with a screaming finale. It was the only aspect of the performance which I expected, since he had pulled that trick on different occasions.

As mentioned above, this tale changed over the years to incorporate other events. Bob told the story as a boy in Edmonds, but his original audience knew he had never lived in Minnesota. His high school students could be taken in by this fiction since they hadn't known him very long.

Supernatural Subtext

Certain factors set this tale apart from other folk narratives. Bob admits that this is largely fictional. He based "The River Boys" on a fragment of a story he heard in summer camp in 1949, when he was eight years old. That elementary original tale dealt with a boy who returned from the dead. Bob fleshed it out with elements of his own life, which gives "The River Boys" a distinctly literary nature. Aside from being a one man play, it is also an oral short story with a supernatural subtext.

The narrator says at the outset that stories protect him from evil. One could easily find a rationalist reason why Bob's bike miraculously veered away from the car. The female witness's input strengthens a supernatural evaluation because she is independent of the narrator. It saves him from directly calling for this conclusion. In the visit to the graveyard, Bob brings up a folk belief that treading on a grave will awaken the buried person. The mysterious deaths of Delano, Bjornson, and Lee give the subtext a menacing quality. Bob implies that some curse, fate, Divine retribution, or Marvin's ghost has killed The River Boys one-by-one; but his own death scene turns that into a joke. It gives the tale literary symmetry by beginning with supernatural rescue and climaxing with supernatural revenge. Moreover, by completing the telling of the story, he has lost that protection.

The tale's real ending comes when Bob resurrects himself, wishes everyone a "pleasant Halloween" and concludes, "If I'm not here on Monday, you'll know why." This goes along with the supernatural subtext, in that the story has not really ended, and the risk remains. Threat assessment expert and celebrity bodyguard Gavin De Becker said that gallows humor about a serious threat is a normal way to convey concern, without showing obvious fear.

Folklore Traditions

The story incorporates other facets of folklore more directly. The first visit to the Haunted House of North Ridge is a legend trip. Folklorist Gary Hall defines this as when a group goes to the site of a local legend. The place then becomes a mood-setting visual aid to enhance the fright factor of a storytelling event. It also combines physical activity with oral tradition. Gary Hall's article, "The Big Tunnel", focuses on the practice as a tradition for teenagers, and as a storytelling aid. Such expeditions are perfectly acceptable for adults. Someone who goes alone on a legend trip will scare himself, but miss out on the camaraderie of a group effort.

Bob's inclusion of a legend trip foreshadows the upcoming tragedy. Delano, Bjornson, and Lee imbue the house with a murderous history, where a psychopath supposedly killed seven people.

The jaunt is appropriate in other traditional ways. Simon J. Bronner's article "Folk Objects" identified haunted houses as, "in a sense, the objective correlatives of fear and wonder of the supernatural." That also applies to the cemetery, which The River Boys visit. The house's location is part of folk narrative traditions, since haunted houses are often located on the edge of town. One should also remember that Bob's father immediately establishes the perilous periphery in North Ridge as the area across the proverbial wrong side of the tracks. The shanty town, as described by Bob, turns the hobos into unseen outsiders, or "others."

Itinerant wanderers have long held a place of suspicion in folk belief–often with good cause. Some folklorists have studied insiders versus outsiders/us-against-them legends in order to unmask the prejudice of tradition bearers. That was the agenda of John Lindow and Timothy Tangherlini.

Hobos are estranged from almost any community, especially ones that value stability, cleanliness, and a profession. The image of a murderous transient is only too believable. Consider the case of Mexican hobo Angel Maturino Resendez alias Rafael Resendez-Ramirez, who rode freight trains around the U.S.A. The FBI added him to the Ten Most Wanted List on June 21, 1999, for murdering eight people in Texas, Illinois, and Kentucky. He later turned himself in, and was executed.

Bob McAllister found a plausible way to cast Marvin's murderer as an outsider, yet not arise from outside the story. The graffiti, bottles, and mattress establish that someone has sheltered himself there. It is conceivable that a drifter or fugitive might hole up in an abandoned house; and no other character in "The River Boys" qualifies as a believable suspect. Bob backs away from directly scapegoating any hobos himself. The narrator leaves that conclusion up to the authorities within the story. He used the same device at the start of "The River Boys", when the witness to the bike incident suggested a supernatural evaluation.

Pranks

"The River Boys" deals largely with pranks, then turns into a prank itself. Folklorist Hennig Cohen set forth in the article "Going to See the Widow" that practical jokes are often a group activity designed to punish an enemy, humble a boaster, or as a form of initiation. Bob and Lee meet through a trick, the theft of the former's prized baseball cap. This also establishes Lee as a future criminal–who loves the thrill of being chased–and initiates Bob as a new neighbor. The River Boys' capers also subvert adult authority, though the practice usually backfires.

Bob has reason for this emphasis. One should consider the usual context of the storytelling session: Halloween in a classroom. Practical jokes are acceptable on festive occasions, like Halloween, April Fool's Day, or the last day of school, but not on any other day. The classroom setting is also important, because the activity should still convey a lesson. Bob remains a teacher first and an entertainer second. Students focus on the action, but one theme warns that practical jokes can cause injury or death. Marvin's fate exemplifies the cruelty of many pranks.

The tale is more dramatic than didactic, so not every listener will pick up on the message. Rather than preach, Bob stresses his own responsibility for Marvin's fictitious death, yet remains a prankster at heart. This Halloween tragedy never happened. The River Boys played tricks in Washington, but never caused the death of Marvin Gorsuch (a real person) nor of anyone else.

The difference between these dangerous pranks and the story/prank is that the latter plays out in a controlled environment. Nobody runs the risk of injury, just of momentary shock from the shrieks of Bob's broad death scene. This manner of trickery is also known as a "Jump Tale", wherein a speaker's delivery of the last line should make the audience jump in terror. Journalist Mary Cronin wrote about a raconteur with this skill in the 1998 *Seattle Times* article "Storyteller Jackie Torrence's Hisses and Howls Will Grab You."

"The River Boys" includes yet another aspect of pranks' effects on people. When the lunatic boy, Aaron, took a hostage, the student body and the narrator himself mistook the incident for a theatrical trick. The title of one *Bainbridge Review* article was, "They thought it was a gag."

The attack took place in the time slot for drama awards. Bob had established a reputation as a prankster, so the on-lookers had grown to expect it of him and his troupe. The tradition turned full circle on the drama teacher and surviving River Boy.

This reaction of laughter from the audience enraged Aaron. He wanted to exploit prank traditions to aid his scheme, but the plan boomeranged on him. The assassin remembered being mocked by the students who apparently thought it was a skit. Aaron later told the state psychologist, "I wanted to show them that this was serious, and not some kind of joke."

The Assassin

Some points in the assassination scene need clarification. Aaron was disarmed by the efforts of principal Dave Ellick, student Dave Prout, teacher Jim Dow, and teacher Bim Prince. Prout was stabbed in the arm, and Ellick's hand was slashed, while the hostage, Julia Thomas, escaped unhurt. The police told Bob of Aaron's threat. I will withhold the attacker's surname, out of consideration for his family.

Bob's audience at our storytelling session knew what the Moving Up assembly was. I did not. At the assemblies, freshmen, sophomores, juniors, and seniors sit in specially designated sections of the gymnasium bleachers, arranged by grade level. My informant later explained that the Moving Up assembly consists of handing out awards for scholastic achievements, with drama prizes presented last. The ceremony ends with seniors leaving their assigned bleacher area, and filing out of the gym. The juniors then "move up" to the vacated section. It is a mild rite-of-passage.

Although "The River Boys" remains fictional, Bob gives a true account of the event of May 27, 1993. I matched that part of his oral tale with newspaper reports, court records, and state psychologist R. M. Hart's interview with Aaron in Western State Hospital in June of 1993. This section of the chapter will demonstrate that the boy's actions are consistent with those of assassin personalities. The motive was all about attention.

Bob characterized Aaron as an introvert. Dr. R. M. Hart called the attacker "a socially isolated young man" with "feelings of failure. "However, the psychologist further reported that Aaron "did report this year feeling, for the first time, some sense of social inclusion as a result of being in Mr. McAllister's class." Aaron also mentioned having previously liked his hostage, Julia Thomas.

Aaron could have ambushed Bob at an accessible, semi-private location such as a parking lot, Bob's office between the chorus room and the stage, or a restroom. The assassin also knew his target's phone number, so he could have tracked him to his home. Then, however, few if anyone would have seen the event. Aaron wanted a big audience.

It is significant that Aaron, a senior, chose an awards ceremony for his stunt. The recipients had earned their merits through hard work in academics, debate, sports, and theater. Obviously, Aaron wasn't picking up any honors himself. He grew steadily angrier as the ceremony progressed, while he watched more and more accolades bestowed upon individuals he envied. Aaron borrowed a Swiss Army knife from his friend, Corey, then tried to build up the "courage" to launch the attack. Bob told us what happened next.

Aaron's bumblings also represent aspects of the assassin personality. Some of these violent attention seekers become mass murderers. FBI behavioral scientist John Douglas defined a mass murderer as someone who kills at least four people in one incident and one particular location. He said in the book *Anatomy of Motive* that a mass killing scenario is all part of a single "emotional experience."

Douglas ran the Behavioral Sciences Unit in Quantico, Virginia for the FBI. Jason Marc Harris and I attended his book signing event at the University Bookstore in Seattle in 1999. He was as charismatic a storyteller as Bob McAllister.

John Douglas and the aforementioned threat assessment expert Gavin De Becker both assert that assassins are usually loners. Mr. De Becker pointed out that such criminals develop a sinister sense of intimacy with their intended victims. This becomes more pronounced in assassins who employ knives, as opposed to guns or bombs. Aaron used a knife.

One wonders why Aaron would lock onto Bob, as opposed to any of the popular honorees. John Douglas maintains that an assassin's crime arises from his emotional development, skills, and interests. Aaron had recently become interested in theater, and had signed up for nearly all of the elective courses taught by Bob. Like other assassins and stalkers, Aaron must have fixated on what his target represented.

When Aaron failed to find his original target, he chose someone else he could control. He singled out Julia Thomas because–in his own words to the state psychologist–"she was close by, and she was small." Aaron was five-foot-five and weighed one hundred and sixty pounds. It seems unlikely that he could have overpowered Bob, who was six-foot-two, and nimble. Then again, nothing else held Aaron back.

A target switch is not unique. Arthur Bremer planned to kill President Nixon, but could never actually reach him. The criminal therefore settled for shooting and crippling a Presidential candidate, Governor George Wallace in 1972. I asked two Secret Service agents about Bremer's parole in 2007. One agent said, "We aren't even watching him anymore." Bremer had lost his notoriety.

Another target switching assassin was John W. Hinckley, Jr. He stalked President Carter to Nashville in 1980, but later opted for a more accessible victim, President Reagan in March of 1981. These two failed assassins, Bremer and Hinckley, had time on their side. They had considerably greater mobility than Aaron. Remember the small scale of Aaron's plot: Bob was the last speaker on the awards list; the would-be killer was obsessed with making a spectacle of himself, but he only had a brief window of opportunity.

Aaron was what Gavin De Becker called an identity seeker with a delusion of identity. The latter, wherein Aaron calls himself the son of Moses would mean

219

he felt a Divine power guided him to achieve a holy objective. Aaron later denied that he meant any of those proclamations. Nothing conveys his desire for attention more than his dramatic exit line, "You'll remember me for this." It helps confirm De Becker & Douglas's profiles of assassins as attention seekers.

For all of Aaron's threats and bravado during his attack, and subsequent police interrogation, the romance soon wore off. The court order, which committed Aaron to the State Hospital for evaluation, indicated that he showed such "signs" as nervousness, crying, and hysteria.

Dr. Hart's interview with Aaron, submitted to the court on June 23, 1993, provides further insight into the boy's mindset. Apparently, the State psychologist knew nothing of Aaron's telephone stalking of Bob. The defendant had previously branded his teacher as Satan before ever referring to him as the Antichrist. Aaron said that his Mormon Bible study class had recently studied Armageddon, so the concept had been on his mind. The boy stated he did not mean any of that nonsense about a mission from God, casting himself as the son of Moses, or viewing Bob as the Antichrist. Dr. Hart believed Aaron's denials and diagnosed him as having an "Adjustment Disorder with Mixed Disturbance of Emotions" instead of a psychosis. The phone calls convinced Bob McAllister otherwise.

Why, then, would Aaron wreck his own defense? If he had stuck to his story, he might have either won acquittal on the basis of insanity, or the judge might have foregone imprisonment in favor of hospitalization. Bob believes that we should look to Aaron's religious convictions. The felonies were bad enough, but he had also committed numerous sins in the process. These included pride and blasphemy, plus acts of violence like holding a woman hostage, and wounding two men with a knife. Aaron could not deny the criminal offenses, but he probably thought he could undo the religious ones. Twenty years in prison might have seemed insignificant compared to an eternity in perdition.

Bob's insights into Aaron are not just because he knew him. John Douglas said at the University Bookstore in 1999, "People ask me, 'What's the closest profession to [FBI] profiler?' I say, 'Public school teacher.'"

Bob McAllister's thorough examination of Aaron's actions and mindset proves Douglas's point. The teacher profiled the student's crime, based on behavior before the spectacle, not just Aaron's own contradictions a few weeks after the fact. Dr. R.M. Hart called Aaron's condition an adjustment disorder, which could apply to any adolescent. Bob seems more accurate, with an assessment of a psychotic episode.

Incidentally, the Antichrist is central to the beliefs of sects who expect Armageddon soon. The First and Second Epistles of St. John contain the only passages in the Holy Bible which use the word Antichrist. The term refers to a category of powerful false prophets who deny the coming of Christ (1 John 2:18, 2:22; 2 John 1:7).

A compelling part of the psychological interview was Aaron's version of how he planned the crime. He reported having fantasized "for years" about committing some "outrageous" acts in front of all his peers. He ruled out the graduation ceremony, since more of his schoolmates would attend the Moving Up assembly.

Dr. Hart asked an important question, which applies to anyone with similar plans: "In your fantasies, how does this turn out? What is going to happen?"

Aaron looked at Dr. Hart "with some surprise" and responded, "I never thought that far. I always quit thinking about it when I was down in front of the people."

The psychologist surmised that Aaron was astonished by the legal consequences of his crime. "At several points, he indicated that he never thought all of this would happen."

This appears to apply to other criminals who have attempted mass killings or assassinations. They expect attention, but do not consider consequences like onerous attorney fees, incarceration, shame, and–like Arthur Bremer–a wasted life of obscurity without accomplishment. They ignore all of that, though they fear failure in their self-appointed mission. Aaron's plans started to unravel when his classmates jeered at him.

Aaron eventually pleaded guilty to two counts of second degree assault with a deadly weapon on David Prout and Julia Thomas. Both victims wanted their attacker to receive psychiatric treatment instead of incarceration. Prout's Victim Impact Statement concluded with, "He's a good kid." Many other people wrote in, asking for leniency. Nevertheless, Aaron drew a two year jail sentence, with credit for 148 days served, plus two years of Community Placement Supervision, and a total of $427 in fines. This was one tenth of the maximum sentence. Aaron paid his last fine, completing his sentence, on August 12, 1997. He was ordered never to make contact again with Dave Prout, David Ellick, Julia Thomas, or Bob McAllister.

Bob heard nothing about the case after that.

Crime

As one can see, crime is crucial to "The River Boys." Apparently, Bob's father in the story had good reason to warn The River Boys about the area by the railroad tracks. He had moved to North Ridge because of the railroad spur, so he already knew about the danger of the location. A criminal, not an evil spirit, killed Marvin. A life of crime brought about Lee Grant's bizarre death. Bob capitalized on the assassination attempt's thematic connection to the fictitious Halloween tale. Supernatural aid and retribution are covert forces within the tale, but criminality poses a tangible threat to one's safety.

Illegality also applies to other folklore genres. Proverbs like "Crime does not pay", "Thieves fall out", "There is no honor among thieves", and "If you can't do the time, don't do the crime" all relate to this issue.

Conspiracy theories swirl around political murders, especially of President Kennedy. Bob's accounts of Aaron's deeds provides more accurate insight into assassin personalities than one finds in any of those dubious hypotheses.

Psychopaths appear in many farfetched urban legends, like "The Hook", which Bob performs as an example of a Halloween tradition. Serial killers, like David "Son of Sam" Berkowitz in New York or the Zodiac Killer in San Francisco, have occasionally preyed upon young couples. Graphic details of these attacks make urban legends look tame in comparison.

The effects of these kinds of predators probably stretch back a long way. Robert Ressler, the FBI profiler who coined the term serial killer in the 1970s, sets forth an interesting folk belief theory. He explained in *I Have Lived in the Monster*. He believes that people in medieval times attributed vicious, incomprehensible killings to werewolves and vampires. Ressler explains: "Supernatural causes, people felt in the era before Freud, were the only logical explanations for excessively savage murders, blood drainings, and other such monstrous acts" (46). This hypothesis proposes a direct link between those supernatural tales and modern urban legends of psychopaths.

Folklorists should learn as much accurate information as possible about crime, which remains a legitimate concern in people's lives. It also provides a wealth of verbal lore.

Conclusion

"The River Boys" has grown from a minimal campfire tale into an oral short story, and solo play. It helps provide insight into presentation, memory theory, threat assessment, folklore's interaction with drama, and the necessity of context dependence. It also shows how the study of one story can lead to the exploration of many folklore issues.

Bob died of cancer in 2014, at the age of seventy-three. He had performed "The River Boys" every Halloween at school, plus as a benefit the Paradise Theater School in Chimacum, Jefferson County, Washington; and at Bainbridge Performing Arts for a special Halloween performance. Matt Hadlock ran the sound system in the latter performance, just as he had done when Aaron tried to take over the Moving Up assembly.

Bob adapted two aspects of "The River Boys" into short stories in *Thief of Hubcaps*. "Indian Bent Pine" about his friendship with Lee Grant; and "Thread" about the stalking done by Aaron. That book was a long overdue volume, preserving the tales Bob had told over the course of his life.

Bob's lore makes many connections. He connected with his students to impart lessons; combined entertainment with disciplined pedagogy; and individual artistic impulse with tradition. In terms of performance, he brought together the art forms of drama, short stories, and personal experience narratives, and Halloween lore within a safe and appropriate setting.

The last of The River Boys has passed away, but the story will live on.

Heidi Jackson, walked down the aisle by her father, Bob McAllister, author of "The River Boys." Taken August 26, 2006

Chapter 5
Four Anti-Memorats

by Gail Duncan, Jay Duncan,
Garrett Vance & Ralph Cheadle
As told to & analyzed by
Birke Duncan

Introduction

This chapter will explore stories by different raconteurs. The first tale arose from a small child's mistaken perception. The next two tales, told by Garrett W. Vance, deal with a Halloween prank, and a case where he mistook an earthquake for a demonic threat. The final tale, told by Ralph Cheadle, describes personal hardships that led to a disturbing mental illusion on a journey. The common thread between these stories is that they are all anti-memorats.

In order to clarify the term, coined by Thomas DuBois in 1998, one must first consider related genres. An anti-tale is a third-person fictional narrative with all the elements of a ghost story, but a sudden plot twist at the end turns it into a joke. That's according to Henning

Sehmsdorf & Reimund Kvideland in *Scandinavian Folk Belief and Legend*. A memorat is a first-hand account of an alleged supernatural encounter. An anti-memorat is therefore a firsthand account which involves mistaken perception of a supernatural presence. The most suspenseful examples incorporate the style, mood, motifs, and structure of ghost stories but turn into non-supernatural anecdotes.

"A Real-Live Leprechaun"

by Gail Duncan and Jay Duncan

My first memorable encounter with this genre was in 1974. My mother came back from lunch at Denny's in Bellevue, Washington. She told us that my youngest brother, two-year-old Jay, had embarrassed her. A little man worked as the busboy at that eatery. Jay exclaimed, "A leprechaun! I see me a real-live leprechaun." The toddler rushed from the booth to ask the restaurant worker where he had concealed his pot of gold. My mother corralled Jay and apologized to the diminutive gentleman.

The small worker said, "That's all right, ma'am. It happens all the time."

As an adult, Jay met Vince DeRubeis from that same neighborhood of Robinswood in Bellevue. Vince, as a tiny child, had mistaken the same little man for a leprechaun, and peppered him with similar questions.

That's not a ghost story, but it shows children's mistaken perception of a real person via fairy lore adapted to illustrated books.

One can usually narrate an anti-memorat with considerably less social risk than a "true" ghost story. The genre calls for little suspension of disbelief on the part of the audience, so the performance does not impeach a storyteller's perception, sanity, or judgment. The performance can also elevate the speaker above the perceived ranks of people who believe they have actually experienced something supernatural.

The three oral tales transcribed for this chapter have an important mutual trait: they build to climaxes rather than anti-climaxes; payoffs instead of let-downs.

Jason Harris and I did not select frightening stories which end with, "Then I woke up" or "I'm only kidding." All narratives make listeners anticipate a funny, scary, or interesting outcome. A memorat leads a listener to a frightening or wondrous conclusion, like the description of seeing a ghost. A successful anti-memorat needs a resolution worthy of its level of suspense, otherwise the audience feels cheated.

At least three kinds of anti-memorats arise in festive storytelling: stories as pranks; stories about pseudo-supernatural hoaxes; and admissions of mistaken perception not necessarily caused by design. The effect of the latter can be frightening or amusing.

This is not a new folklore topic. For instance, St. John Seymour and Harry Neligan explored "Mistaken Identity" tales as a chapter in their 1914 book, *True Irish Ghost Stories*. They catalogued some accounts of hoaxes and honest mistakes. Washington Irving's 1810 short story, "The Legend of Sleepy Hollow" relies upon the premise of a hoax based on a local folk belief. Images of hoodwinking the credulous through counterfeit hauntings are commonplace in folk narrative, literature, and other forms of entertainment. But even if the issue itself is not new, this is the first presentation and examination of the following three stories in print.

Pranks

The chapter about "The River Boys" already explained the dynamics of first person stories as pranks. Unlike memorats, they can be entirely fictitious and end as jump tales. Not all jump tales qualify as anti-memorats, since many of them function in the third person.

A first person narrative about a prank is another matter entirely. The speaker tells of how he led someone else, or a group, into a mistaken perception of a supposed supernatural incident; a dupe tells of being tricked; someone boasts of foiling a prank, etc. One can find many possible points of view.

Participation in pseudo-supernatural practical jokes does not preclude belief. Such is the case with the champion ghost story teller, Garrett Vance. His lifelong belief in ghosts does not discourage him from telling anti-memorats, or playing tricks.

One such story illustrates that point. This time, the pivotal character is not Garrett, but his younger brother Norman D. Vance.

Garrett accurately described Norman as a mad genius, with a talent for creating gizmos. Among other things, the younger Vance brother made his own toy laser gun, which could light up and emit beeps.

In addition to his inventions, Norman was also a self-styled master of disguise. His masterpiece was when he walked the streets of Bainbridge Island in the guise of a World War I soldier, complete with combat boots, leggings, high collared uniform, and vintage wide brimmed steel helmet.

I missed the time when Norman combined costuming with amateur gadgetry, but it happened to be appropriate for this study. Garrett first told me the tale during a ferry ride to Seattle, when his brother was the topic of our conversation. We recorded the following presentation on May 8, 1997, at one o'clock, in Garrett's Seattle apartment. Before narration began, I reminded him that I had not attended the party on Halloween of 1982.

"The Halloween Prank"

by Garrett Vance

"You missed a really fun story," said Garrett, "Now you'll get to hear it. You'll feel as if you were there.

"It was at my house which is on the north end of Bainbridge Island in Puget Sound over on the beach. We were doing *Rossum's Universal Robots*, and it was the cast party. I was the Student Director [assistant to director Bob McAllister], and Birke here was one of the mad doctors.

"It started about four o'clock or so." The final performance of the play had been a Sunday matinee. "Everybody came over, and we ate lots of candy and popcorn, and Coca Cola, and got all hyperactive and incoherent.

"As it started to get darker, my brother Norman disappeared from the proceedings. He was hanging out, too, because he was one of the stage crew boys. He disappeared. I didn't notice. I was standing by the window with Andy Rostrand, and we were looking out at the water. Out of the corner of my eye, I saw movement. I said, 'What was that?'

"I see this black shadow kind of going down under the bank. I said to myself, 'Uh-oh. Norman is up to something. I'll keep Andy here talking and we'll see what Norman does next.'

I said, 'Hey, Andy, look at the view. Isn't the water nice? It's beautiful, even in the gray.'

"'Sure.'

"The next thing we know, we see a black shadow jump from behind a maple tree, down below the grass bank.

"Andy said, 'Hey, what was that?'

"I said, 'What?'--even though I saw it, too.

"'Well, I saw a shadow. I saw a black billowing shadow'--because there was a cape-'like jump from the maple tree down the bank.'

"'What? No way.'

"'Well, I'm sure I saw it.'

"I said, 'Oh, you're just spooked. It's Halloween. Ha, ha, ha, ha!'

"We kept talking. The next thing we knew, I saw this little, black-hooded head pop up from the edge of the bank. Andy said, 'Look! Look!'

"I said, 'Where? Where?'

"I'm looking the wrong way. Out of the corner of my eye, I saw Norman pull his head back a little bit. He had his face all blacked out; and there were just two red, glowing eyes. He had put little LEDs [light-emitting diodes] with the batteries in there.

"I know my brother. I know what he's up to. Andy doesn't know. Andy suddenly sees this little demon face pop up, with glowing eyes. Andy just went like this: 'AAAAH!'

"Norman was smart; he quickly went back down again.

"I said, 'What, what, what?'

"Andy said, 'I saw it! I saw it! And it had red eyes!'

"'What? You're crazy. No way.'

"'No, I saw it.' He was really spooked.

"Norman stayed away. He hid.

"Meanwhile, Andy's circulating the party, telling everybody that he saw this shape. People are saying, 'Oh, Andy's a pretty honest kid. He thought he saw something.'

"He spread the story. I talked to people, too: 'Well, Andy thought he saw something out there. You know, there are some Indian ghosts around here, and a lot of legends.'

"I was building it up.

"They were saying [shakily]: 'Oh, okay, okay.'

"By then it was dark. Somebody said, 'Let's tell ghost stories.'

"I said, 'Yeah, yeah.'

"Well, I wanted to save mine for later. So I said, 'Well, hey, I have a record of ghost stories.'

"I had some spooky eighth grade record. I put that on [spooky music imitation]:"'Wooh, oooh, ooh, ooooooh.' And then came the ghost stories. It was like 'The Golden Arm', 'The Phantom Train', and 'The Monkey's Paw.'

"It's all dark. We turned out all the lights. Everybody's lying and lounging around on the living room floor. The record player's going. I'm sitting right in the middle, on the floor. And I'm looking up to the windows, because I know what is going to happen. Heh, heh, heh! We're listening to the record, and I hear scratching on the glass." Garrett ran his fingernails down the window. "I can't do it, but [it was] this kh-kh-kh-kh scratching on the glass. And I'm thinking [softly]: 'Here he comes.'

"Kh-kh-kh-kh-kh.

"People are saying, 'Hey, did you hear something outside?'

"I'm saying, 'Oh, no. Huh-uh.'

"Kh-kh-kh.

"They're saying, 'Oh, gee, I heard something.'

"I said, 'No, no. Probably just some branches on the glass.'

"Then I heard this thump on the deck. I look over at Andy in the dimness of the LEDs on the stereo, and his eyes are as big as saucers. He's like [stage whisper]: 'I hear something out there.'

"Heh, heh, heh! Everybody's starting to get spooked out.

"'It's nothing. Listen to the story.'

"The room has gotten a little unnerved now. They're all hyper-aware.

"We hear this skittering sound–kch-kch-sh-sh– going across, out in front.

"They say, 'We heard that. We heard that.'

"I said, 'It's a raccoon. It's nothing.'

"'Are you sure?'

"'Yeah, I'm sure.'

"Everybody's looking at me. Right then, out of the window–obviously the tape can't see my body movements–but from a bent down position, all of a sudden, Norman raised up with his black garments; and his cape waved in the breeze. He was this huge black shadow against the window. His eyes are glowing red. And he howled [for six seconds]: 'OOOH, OOOH, OOOH, OOOOOH, AH, AH!'

"The room became a roiling bucket of snakes. Everybody was trying to get away from the window as fast as they could, and were crawling over other people. I was in the middle of it. Fourteen girls and ten guys were screaming: 'AAAH!' Norman's banging on the glass: kuh, kuh, kuh! [Garrett bangs on his apartment window] 'Let me in!'

"His eyes are glowing red.

"Andy can't even scream. He's just: [mouth open, strangled cry.] I'm laughing because all these girls are crawling over me. I'm getting breasts and thighs in my face.

"'WAAH!'

"They're all running away. They're back in the bathroom, and they're screaming, yelling. And I'm just: 'Bah, ha, ha, ha, ha!'--dying of laughter.

"Finally, Norman couldn't take it anymore. He started to laugh. Somebody turned on the lights and the scare was over. Norman and I did a big old high five. Heh, heh, heh, heh, heh, heh! So that was the story."

"Now tell me," I asked, "were they mad at you?"

"No, they loved it."

"They did?"

"It was a Halloween party. What the hell?"

Before continuing with analysis, the reader deserves an epilogue. Norman D. Vance joined the Army in 1987, at the age of nineteen. The master of disguise marched in a Fort Lewis Veterans Day parade in his own World War I uniform. Norman served for twenty years as a topography teacher and drill instructor. He retired as a Sergeant, and moved to Molokai, Hawaii.

Andy Rostrand and Garrett Vance remained close friends for the next thirty years. Andy passed away from a heart attack in 2013, at the age of 48, mourned by his wife and friends.

Analysis

We seriously considered omitting this funny tale of teenagers goofing off. Jason Harris and I kept the yarn because it adds a dimension to Garrett's storytelling range, and clarifies an aspect of folk belief.

"The Halloween Prank" is part of Garrett's repertoire of campfire ghost stories. Unlike full-fledged memorats, this anecdote remains appropriate for other occasions as well, such as reminiscences of amateur theatricals, Halloween parties, or his brother's disguises and gizmos.

The Vance brothers' Halloween trick was skillful, scary, but relatively safe. They did not try it on the beach, nor on anyone in a moving car. Garrett & Norman targeted the victims in an enclosed space, then stopped the hysteria before it got out of hand. The hosts created a situation where the guests were receptive to a ghostly event. Of course, the calendar was on their side since scary tricks are appropriate on Halloween night.

The choice of victims was also socially acceptable. The Vance brothers picked on members of their age-peer group, not on children–which would have been emotionally abusive– nor on adults–bullying mixed with rebellion. The targets were also fellow thespians, so the costume and Garrett's indoor lighting effects were related to theater.

Part of how Garrett tricks the guest into anxiety is by alluding to community legends. The main Native American legend was of a Suquamish tribe drunkard, who had slit a man's throat in order to steal his whiskey. The killer became the only person executed by public hanging in Port Madison. That was in 1877. One can find the account in the archives of the Bainbridge Island Historical Museum.

Garrett also says that he wanted to tell his campfire yarns after Norman's prank: "I wanted to save mine for later." He would have been referring at that time to "The

Story of the *Standard*", about the fishing vessel that sailed away on its own, and returned for its owner's burial.

This was the reason for retaining "The Halloween Prank" in this chapter. Pseudo-supernatural pranks and experience-centered supernatural belief tales are complementary, in this case, not mutually exclusive.

Mistaken Perceptions

This is what comes of creating false impressions in other people, but Garrett tricked himself ten years later. An anti-memorat can be a case wherein the admission of an error in perception amuses other people.

I heard Garrett telling this narrative a couple of times at get-togethers. The two of us recorded this tale shortly after "The Halloween Prank."

"The Earthquake in Japan"

by Garrett W. Vance

"I was in Yokohama, Japan. It was summertime. It was really hot out. I was lying up in the loft, where I had my bed. I had to go up a ladder to get there. It was about ten feet up.

"I was reading with the fan on, while reading H.P. Lovecraft. He was a very strange cat, and it was creepy stuff: 'The Call of Cthulhu.' It was pretty late, about two in the morning. Finally, I couldn't keep my eyes open any more. I thought [moan]: 'Oh, this is really just enough of this.'

"I put the Lovecraft book down beside my futon, and I turned off the light. Well, not three seconds later, the futon began to shake. All the light fixtures shook. I opened my eyes: 'Oh! Oh!'

"I thought Cthulhu was rising from his undead sleep, to get me. That's the first thing. I mean, all of a sudden your bed starts to shake. I thought of *The Exorcist*. I'm like: 'Oh, no. No!'

"Well, the next thing I knew I was on the floor down below. I don't remember getting down. I either teleported, flew, or somehow went down the ladder. Then I realized, 'It's an earthquake.'

"The next thing I know, I'm outside. The ground is still moving, but it's tapering off. It was really shaking. I'm outside, and I'm like [relieved]: 'Oh, that was freaky. That was scary. I'm glad it's over.'

"That was when I realized I was completely naked, out in the street. Then I thought, 'I'd better get back inside.'

"Everybody else slept through it. I don't think anyone saw me, but it was yet another shock. For about two or three seconds, I thought something supernatural was happening."

Analysis

Garrett tells this anti-memorat whenever earthquakes come up in conversation. However, as with jokes and riddles, anecdotes are not reusable on the same audience, unless requested. Earthquakes are a frequent topic in our region, because Washington State lies on the Ring of Fire of seismic and volcanic activity, which encircles the Pacific Ocean. Furthermore, news media report heavily on these disasters. Temblors are far more common in Japan than in Washington State, which explains why Garrett alone dashed out of the house. Shaking ground was as normal to Yokohama neighbors as wind blowing.

Many people tell anecdotes about mistaking an earthquake for something prosaic, like a cat under one's chair or a passing truck. Garrett had put himself in the mindset of malevolent forces by reading a scary book in bed, and memories of a repellent film.

Audiences laugh at this anecdote, even if they have not read any Lovecraft stories. Those who have perused "The Call of Cthulhu" will note that Garrett's experience mirrors the story, which deals with a cosmic god-monster who waits to rule the world again. An earthquake marks the rise of Cthulhu's necropolis from the southern Pacific Ocean. In an example of the Jungian theory of the collective subconscious, the demon invades the dreams of artistic people. Garrett is artistic, and had just been reading the story, so the context of a real temblor makes his half-awake assumption seem almost logical.

This is also why audiences identify with the story. Anyone who watches a horror movie or reads a thriller has placed himself in an emotional state where he can become easily spooked, especially at night.

Garrett reaches three different levels of fear: brief fear of the imaginary entity; fear of a natural disaster; and fear of embarrassment. His nudity comes as a surprise and not a non sequitur, since he emphasizes the summer heat, early in the story. This is an example of good comedic structure. According to TV comedy writer and educator Danny Simon, a funny outcome in a comedy must come from within the boundaries of the story itself.

This tale allows the narrator to amuse audiences, at his own expense. It also pays tribute to H.P. Lovecraft's ability to inspire terror.

Scary Anti-Memorats

The story of "The Earthquake in Japan" has a funny effect, but an anti-memorat can be as disturbing as any ghost story. At least when one reads a memorat, one can comfort oneself by not believing it. Disbelief is emotionally satisfying. Psychological security reigns if one does not believe in superior space aliens who can conquer earth; ghosts that take over houses; fairies who lure people into a parallel universe; etc.

A scary story about a mistaken perception can involve an involuntary hallucination from a psychotic episode, a seizure, or delirium. Jason Harris and I will ignore any tales of drug use and concentrate instead on an incident which came naturally, and by accident.

Back in 1983, Bainbridge High School English teacher Ralph K. Cheadle told a firsthand account to his Early American Literature students. We were discussing a scene in our assigned reading from *The Scarlet Letter*. Chapter 11 "The Interior of a Heart" describes how Reverend Arthur Dimmesdale, who has fathered a child by a married parishioner, flogs himself with a scourge, fasts, and keeps lonely vigils until he endures visions of his secret shame. These include angels, devils, his late parents, and deceased friends. The final image portrays his illegitimate daughter's mother, pointing out Dimmesdale as the seducer.

Our teacher explained that such combined factors as sleep deprivation, isolation, distress, and hunger can cause mental illusions. First, Cheadle cited rituals where shamans retreated into nature, staying awake and unfed for days at a time, until they had a vision.

Mr. Cheadle could relate to it. The forty-three-year-old instructor told a short version of an adventure he had twenty years before. Obviously, I was in no position to transcribe it at the time. The account lingered in my mind for almost sixteen years, until this study came about.

I called the retired teacher and we set up an appointment for August 31, 1999, at one o'clock in the afternoon. He met me in front of the Eagle Harbor Bookstore, and we drove to the Public House bar and grill for lunch. After the following transcription, I will compare this long version to his previous, expurgated account:

"Mr. Cheadle's Hallucinations"

by Ralph Cheadle

"I'm trying to remember exactly," said Mr. Cheadle. Do you want to hear about Mexico?"

"Mexico is fine."

"It was the first time I had been south of a border town. I was with this girl I had met at [The International] Summer School in Oslo. We left her car in Puerto Penasco. She left her guitar in the back of the car, when we took the train to Guaymas. When we got back, the guitar exploded in the heat.

"This was in the summer of '63. I remember that on the train to Guaymas, we couldn't sit together because it was very crowded with a lot of Mexican peons in their white shirts, with their straw hats. I was seated next to an Indian boy. He was about sixteen years old. He was going down to Mexico City. And I remember it was so hot crossing the desert in this train, all the windows were open. This Indian kid was hanging out the window, and I heard a loud *thwack!* early in the morning. I looked over, and he had gone limp and was hanging out. I grabbed him, and pulled him in. A giant June bug had hit him in the head and knocked him unconscious [chuckle].

"Anyway, Then we got to the coast. It was a little resort area, and I got badly sunburned. As an antidote to the painful sunburn, I stayed in the hotel bar and drank. Susan, the girl I was with, wanted to see some more of the beaches. She hitchhiked, got picked up by a Mexican who took her to a very exclusive beach, where he proceeded to have his way with her.

"She returned, very distraught, to the hotel. We left the next day. She was upset and wanted to return home to Berkeley. My car was in Ciudad Juarez or across the border in El Paso. We parted company. It sounds like I parted company with Susan without any real concern for her traumatized condition. I was concerned. And by the time we got to El Paso, it was all right, in my estimation and hers, that she should go on home alone.

"I was sort of meandering back north to Seattle. I wanted, after a while, to return to Mexico, but I only had twenty dollars.

"On the way to Reno, I was sleeping on the side of the road, out in the desert somewhere. It was about three in the morning. I was in my red Volkswagen bug. I woke up. I don't know what it was that had awakened me. It was a two lane highway, but there was very little traffic at that hour of the morning. All of a sudden, something caught my attention to the east, and a rocket took off. And there was this fiery trail as this rocket went up. It seemed like it was thirty yards, but it must have been half a mile away. But it was enormous; it was loud; it was terrifying. Just having awakened, I didn't know where I was. That sort of set the tenor for the rest of the trip home.

"I got into Reno, late the following morning, with my twenty dollars in my pocket, and decided to play blackjack –which was the only game of chance I knew–in one of the casinos, hoping to make enough to finance a return to Mexico.

"I watched the tables in the blackjack section. I saw this guy who looked like a logger. He had black, highwater pants, wool socks, slippers, and braces. He went up to the table and tipped all of the chairs, which I guess was an indication that he was going to play the house alone for big stakes, and he wanted to close the table. I watched him lose over a thousand dollars in fifteen minutes. I remember thinking that this was probably my table. The house gods had exacted their fair share, and would be ready to give.

"I was cleaned out in less time than with the logger. I was virtually penniless; I guess I had some change. I was certainly not going to be able to return to Mexico. I figured I had to get out of Reno; I couldn't pay for any kind of lodging. I drove out, slept again in the car on the side of the road. The next day, I woke up. I'm still in Nevada."

The waitress returned to our table with the beer Mr. Cheadle had ordered. I reached for the pause button. My informant smirked and asked, "You're not going to waste any tape, are you?"

He resumed the story: "I was almost out of gas. That 1961 Volkswagen bug did not have a gas gauge. It had a reserve tank, which had one gallon, which meant you had about thirty miles. I had gone onto reserve.

"I got to this junction which had a small grocery store and gas station. I went in and asked if I could clean up around the place for a tank of gas, do some work, whatever work they had to do: yard work, some work at the grocery, or whatever. They came up with a couple of jobs. I picked up rocks out of a patch of ground they were going to cultivate into a garden. I remember hosing down the concrete area around the pumps. I was given a gallon of gas, which didn't cost much back then. Of course, it was a ten gallon tank.

"I headed north again. I drove all night. By this time, I had made it into southern Idaho. I was out of gas and very hungry. I pulled up to a restaurant, went in, and tried the same story: that I would do dishes for food. I was laughed off and told that if I didn't have money, they weren't interested in my company; and I left.

He paused. "I'm trying to think of where I was. I wish I could remember the names of the towns. If I looked at a map, I could probably figure it out. I should have done that.

"The long and short of it is that I felt I had to keep going, which meant if I slept I would be on the road longer, and without food longer. It was becoming paramount that I get home. At this time, I shifted my destination from Seattle to Spokane, where my parents lived. I went to college in Seattle.

"I went to another rural gas station, and they said they had no work. I guess I appealed to the old guy–and he was quite old–who was the owner and operator of this rural station. I gave him my driver's license, he took down my name and address, and I promised to send the money, and he filled my tank. I was on the road again.

"By this time, I think I had been two nights without sleep. I was very hungry, and I was still in Idaho, going

258

through the mountains northwest of Boise. It was at that time that I began to hallucinate. The pine trees along the road seemed to be stooping over and grabbing at my Volkswagen. I found myself swerving to avoid their grasp. I was going into an extreme panic, and I decided, 'Well, I at least need food.'

"I stopped at a restaurant which was sort of a mountain pass lodge. I went in and told them my story. I must have looked hollow eyed and wan, because they took pity, fed me a hamburger and fries."

Our meal arrived on cue. I asked if we could break for lunch, and he agreed, but Mr. Cheadle soon brought up something else of interest. I turned the recorder back on.

"At one point, I was at a service station. It may have been the one where I succeeded in working for the fuel. I had actually had the gas pump speaking to me. Do you remember that? Did I say that? Yeah.

"At the time I had been reading–have you heard of Alan Watts?" He was a British-American philosopher. "He wrote a lot about Zen Buddhism. I had been reading a lot of Alan Watts. He had also written a lot about various mystics, so I was really trying for some kind of metaphysical experience. And that's then the gas pump spoke to me. I couldn't decipher what it said. It wasn't necessarily in a language I didn't understand. It was at a level, I guess.

"That's pretty much it. I made it home after that bum meal in the mountain pass."

I asked, "When did you realize you were hallucinating about the trees?"

"After eating that last borrowed meal. By the way, I made all of those borrowed meals & borrowed fuel good. I kept the addresses, borrowed money from my father, made good those debts quickly with interest, then repaid my father.

"It was after that introduction of some food that I realized what I experienced was entirely hallucination. Of course, that didn't minimize the fear or panic, because it was absolutely real at the time."

260

I inquired: "Did it affect your beliefs in any way, after that?"

"Well, the talking gas pump did tug at my orthodoxy, which at that time was purely Protestant. I never did, as I said, decipher the message of the gas pump. It was a mind altering, mind expanding experience. As a result of that, I've become more open to experiences in a spiritual way."

We later finished our meal and the waitress brought the check. I took out my wallet, but Mr. Cheadle said, "Don't touch your money. This is on me."

Contexts

The version Mr. Cheadle told in class in 1983 was context dependent. Since it illustrated a point in our reading assignment, he omitted all of the events in Mexico and instead took up with the action on his arrival in Reno. He did not mention the lumberjack, either. The narrator condensed the story of the trip back to Washington, and ended the tale with the trees grabbing down at his car.

The image certainly made an impression on me. I remember discussing it later with a few classmates. We found it fascinating and disturbing, because any one of us could have wound up under similar circumstances.

The second context, nearly sixteen years later, lent itself to a more complete narrative. This time, it was a one-on-one meeting between two adults in a restaurant. My chief worry was that the din of other patrons' chatter, and silverware clinking on plates would drown out the narrator's voice. Our mutual adult status also meant that Mr. Cheadle did not need to expurgate the story. In 1983, he had excised Susan altogether.

Time constraint also plays a part in storytelling. Our Early American Literature class lasted forty-five or fifty minutes per day. The narrator truncated the narrative, so as not to stray too far from the discussion of the reading assignment. In 1999, Mr. Cheadle was retired from thirty years of teaching English at Bainbridge High School. In a pub, with no job to get back to, he had all the time he needed to tell the tale completely.

Analysis

The anti-memorat pattern starts fairly early in Mr. Cheadle's vacation horror story. The narrator sets up the listener or reader for a horrifying vision, but reveals it as a mistaken perception. The first hint of the structure occurs on the train when Mr. Cheadle hears the noise and his seatmate goes limp. One imagines that the peon boy had hit a telephone pole, expecting the narrator to say, "I pulled him in, and his head was gone." I was relieved to hear otherwise. If Mr. Cheadle had not taken action, the young Mexican might have tipped out of the moving train. The narrator's rescue of another human being was the only thing that went right on this trip.

Susan's victimization follows a more predictable pattern. She was alone, in a foreign country, engaged in a high risk activity. According to Sanford Strong's crime prevention book, *Strong on Defense* the three factors which aid a predator most are "time, isolation, and control" (50). The rapist was in the ideal position to transport Susan to a lonely place, where he had power.

The rest of the story returns to anti-memorat mode. The rocket scene reminds one of UFO stories, except Mr. Cheadle immediately recognized the sight as a man-made device.

The casino scene is especially interesting. The logger's behavior exemplifies post-payment actions of men in dangerous, far-from-home occupations. Oftentimes, cowboys, fishermen, lumberjacks, and the like collect their pay in a lump sum and then waste it in a spree of gambling, alcohol, parties, etc. It's the origin of the expression, "Spending like a drunken sailor."

This tale deals with what led to an illusory vision, but it also follows the pattern of a memorat. Lauri Honko points out in "Memorates and Folk Belief," norm violation leads to supernatural encounters. Mr. Cheadle violated a norm: he gave in to temptation in Reno, which complicated an already troubled situation. The story now takes on cautionary overtones about repercussions of gambling while it ties into the memorat tradition. Henning Sehmsdorf and Reimund Kvideland said in *Scandinavian*

Folk Belief & Legend that card-playing has been seen as a way to invoke supernatural evil (19).

This is also a coming-of-age story . The location of Mr. Cheadle's vision sheds some light on the naturalist theory. A forest would not necessarily seem overtly magical, under ordinary circumstances, but it becomes ominous when one feels vulnerable. Ralph Cheadle was overwhelmed by his physical, financial, and emotional hardships.

The story served a purpose in context by explicating a scene in the reading assignment, and introduced students to the dynamics of an ancient mythical practice. Cheadle's account maintains rationalism, disturbs an audience, and connects to older memorat traditions. The climactic scene with the trees is frightening in two ways: the image projects horror on its own, but Mr. Cheadle's evasive swerves could have killed him or someone else.

We noticed that the narrator jumbles the chronology near the end, regarding the talking gas pump.

His mental state would undoubtedly affect his ordering of the events, after the fact. The story has developed a nightmarish tone.

The talking gas pump moves the story close to memorat status. He believes his fatigue placed him at a different level of consciousness. Mr. Cheadle subsequently used the experience in terms of being more open to different cultures' beliefs, as opposed to writing off others' experiences as hallucinatory.

Tree Lore

My co-author Jason Harris observed something important about the story. Mr. Cheadle's anti-memorat shares some aspects with memorats and mythic rituals, but it also intersects with another tradition: fairy tales.

Cheadle's story is not the first to deal with sinister trees. Kathrine Briggs pointed out on page 197 of *A Dictionary of Folk-Tales in the English Language*, "Traditions of malignant and benevolent trees are widespread in England, but are hardly treated in the Motif-

Index." Mr. Cheadle's hallucination is a variant of Motif F402.6.1 "Demon lives in tree."

My informant's account shares features with an English fairy tale, "Crooker", collected by Ruth Tongue. In that story, a nameless traveler hikes at twilight toward a village called Cromford, in Derbyshire, in order to visit his sick mother. He meets three green-clad fairy women at different junctures along the way. They all warn the traveler, separately, about "Crooker", and give him posies of flowers as magical protection: St. John's Wort, primroses, and daisies respectively. Each charm comes to him as a reward for three previous rescues of animals from traps: a bird, a rabbit, and a fox.

It turns out that Crooker is an ash tree, which breaks the necks of wayfarers at night, then hurls them into the enchanted Darrent or Derwent River. The tree's name arises from its crooked shadow which appears to extend "skinny, clutching hands." The frightened traveler decides to run past Cromford Bridge and "for all his weariness, he did" (196).

As he progresses toward the stone bridge, he hears the river's babblings pronounce the word, "Hungry." The traveler sees the pursuing "shadow of long crooked hands, like branches." First he throws daisies over his left shoulder, and the shadow disappears. When the presence reappears, he throws primroses over his left shoulder, and stops Crooker again. The traveler continues running, but the "clutching shadow" bars his way. He hurls St. John's Wort straight at the tree and leaps onto the bridge. The tree shrieks, the river roars and moans.

Meanwhile, Cromford villagers recognize the noises and surmise that Darrent River and Crooker have claimed another victim. They don't dare venture out until daylight. When they do, they find the traveler alive, praying at the bridge's shrine (196-197).

We see some interesting similarities between this fairy tale and the anti-memorat. "Crooker" could not have affected Mr. Cheadle's narrative, but they both had a common influence. It is normal for people to pick out human-like silhouettes of hands and facial profiles in the outlines of trees. A troubled observer could easily view these images as sinister.

An oblique and unintentional continuity is the donor motif. The traveler receives his protective flowers from dryads or fairies, as rewards for rescuing animals from traps. The animals were probably the fairies in shifted shapes. That coincides with the Motif-Index F330 "Grateful Fairies" and F350 "Gifts from Fairies." Mr. Cheadle rescued the unconscious Mexican boy, teetering out the open window of a moving train. Several days and many miles to the north, when Mr. Cheadle desperately needed food and gasoline, a few generous people helped him. However, this story draws no connection between saving the injured boy and Motif Q10 "Deeds rewarded" or Q40 "Kindness rewarded." They happen to follow a similar pattern.

The meals and gasoline were a straight bartering of goods for services, which Mr. Cheadle honored as loans. The protective elixir here was when the "bum meal" of a burger and fries brought Ralph Cheadle out of his delirious state long enough to realize that the trees had not consciously set out to grab his car. He no longer suffers from terrifying visions. Even the reality-challenging talking gas pump comes across as benign.

Other common points arise between "Crooker" and "Mr. Cheadle's Hallucination." The traveler and Mr. Cheadle were both tired and alone at the perilous periphery, when they evaded the trees' clutches. The English story, however, eliminates all ambiguity because the villagers know of Crooker and Darrent River's lethal history.

Another source influenced Mr. Cheadle's presentation. Back in 1983, he mentioned that his hallucination looked like something out of a movie. The best example of this motif on film is in the 1939 version of *The Wizard of Oz* when Dorothy and the Scarecrow find an orchard of surly, semi-human apple trees. Film disseminated a fantastic image, which affected a folk narrative performance. Yet while Mr. Cheadle did not say that motion pictures inspired his vision, he gave his audience a common reference point in order to visualize the scene.

Conclusion

Anecdotes of pranks and mistaken perceptions are appropriate in many contexts, since they are entertaining and require no suspension of disbelief. Jump tales, on the other hand, are best suited to Halloween and ghost story sessions. A fright factor plays a part in the genre, but anti-memorats lend themselves well to humor. The narrator runs no risk of looking superstitious, gullible, or mentally ill.

Festive anti-memorats, on their own, uphold a rational worldview amid ghost story traditions. Both narrators recognized their anecdotes as continuities of supernatural belief tales. When taken in the context of an entire repertoire, such as with Garrett Vance, anti-memorats do not contradict a tradition bearer's overall beliefs in the supernatural. Rationalists and believers can appreciate the entertainment value of this genre.

Ralph Cheadle and his son, Lucas Cheadle, on Bainbridge
Island, WA.

Miscellaneous Pictures

Jason Harris, Filmmaker Zach Hibbard and Birke Duncan,
Melbourne Independent Filmmakers Festival, 2011.

Garrett Vance and friend, Ingrid Selfors, on the Vance property, Port Madison, Bainbridge Island, Washington, around 1990. This campfire setting was where Garrett told many ghost stories.

"Princess & the Troll Suitors" by John Bauer

"Workers" by Arthur Rackham

Folklorist Birke Duncan in 2006, visiting Lake Yngern, Sweden, scene of "The Troll Tale." Photo courtesy of Hjalmar Olsson.

Folklorist Jason Marc Harris, Ph.D.

Chapter 6
Shadows of Tradition:
The Role of Belief and the
Mechanics of Legend in
Tales of the Spirit World

by Jason Marc Harris

"We never really believed it,
but it was definitely there."

By far, the most prevalent subject of the memorates and legends that Birke Duncan and I collected here in the Northwest was the ghost story. There are several good reasons for this, and I believe that the words of the informants themselves offer ample evidence for the following conclusion: in a word, belief is the issue. This is not to say that all our informants share a belief in ghosts, but rather that everyone seems to have an opinion as to whether or not ghosts exist. "Do you believe in ghosts?" It's a question that people will ask each other–a far more common question than whether fairies or trolls exist, at least here in the Northwestern United States. According to a Gallup Poll, October 1999, "33% of Americans said they believe in ghosts [...] over half–54%--of those 18-29 say they believe in ghosts, compared to only 8% of senior citizens 65 and older." [1] This study reveals how the relation between tradition-bearers and belief is far more complicated than a matter of simple affirmations or denials recorded in a poll. Our informants' tales and comments on belief demonstrate how people are developing their metaphysical impressions and theories from a range of cultural material, and maintaining traditions despite tensions between belief and disbelief.

The growing belief in ghosts by younger people is chiefly a testament to the influence of popular media, rather than oral tradition–notably our informants mention films such as *The Exorcist* and *Poltergeist*. The media, however, is not the only cultural source that presents us with images of a longstanding and powerful belief–or at least–in the afterlife and thus, ghosts. Judging from the Old Testament account of the Witch of Endor, who raises the prophet Samuel from the dead (1 Samuel 28:7-25), and the Greek Epic The Odyssey, where Odysseus descends into the underworld to consult the shade of the prophet

Tiresias, is clear that ghosts have occupied a central place in the anthropological conception of death since antiquity. Folklore abounds with ghosts. There does not seem to be a single culture to which the idea of ghosts is wholly alien.

Other Entities

Besides ghost stories, our informants had tales of other spiritual beings, such as the doppelganger, the nightmare or incubus, and even more demonic manifestations. Notably, there are accounts of fairies here as well. I keep these fairy stories in this context because they emerge from the same legend-telling sessions that presented ghost stories. Furthermore, the informants' statements concerning the fairies are instructive regarding matters of belief. Because of the preponderance of ghost stories and the fact that we do have ghost legends as well as memorates, I focus primarily on that material for this chapter. However, to give a more inclusive view of the traditional material that people tell here in the Northwest, I include some miscellaneous tales of spiritual beings. Indeed, the line between a "ghost," and a "demon," or even a "fairy" is an ambiguous one. Katharine Briggs has noted for example that fairies in many cases seem to be the spirits of the dead.

² Likewise, a "demon" sometimes seems to be an especially unpleasant ghost.

³ Or, a "ghost" may in fact represent some entity that was previously considered a divinity, but whose status has diminished through time and inattention.

⁴ Thus, another reason for the large amount of ghost tales is that people tend to reduce over time any local spiritual tradition to a ghost story. Ghosts are levelers.

For convenience, this chapter is divided into different sections. First, I present some of the transcripts of our various informants, which include some brief commentary by Birke Duncan and me. After the transcripts, an extended analysis follows. The main questions here are: how does the material connect to the popular media, literature, and tradition? What are some functions and structural features of these legends and memorates? What is the relationship between the informants' attitude or belief and the narrative?

In addition to accounts of spiritual beings, I include reports of "second sight." Indeed, in many traditions no one can see a ghost unless they have this supernatural vision. Under the heading of ghosts, you will find "wraiths" as well–the manifestation of an apparition of someone who usually has died at that very moment. Ghosts, second sight, and wraiths inhabit tales that circulate concerning spiritual reality that penetrates the material world that we behold every day.

In our empirical, scientific era, we supposedly live in a time of "seeing is believing." However, the testimony of our informants indicates that belief is not a simple matter of affirmation or denial based on observation alone. Instead, there exists a variety of stances of belief that are the result of a complicated relationship between contemporary culture, individual psychology, religious doctrine, and folkloric tradition.

The Transcripts

Birke Duncan and I interviewed and recorded numerous accounts of contacts with denizens of the otherworld. I have specified which sessions Birke has assisted in transcribing. In several cases, due to spatial limitations, I have resorted to summary. I have organized the following transcripts according to thematic material:

Legendary ghosts

Ouija boards

Family ghosts

Doubles, including Doppelganger, Fetch, & Wraith

Second sight

However, I have generally tried not to disturb the integrity of a storytelling session by slicing and dicing material simply to attach it to a particular heading Thus, beginning for example with Birke's own tales, we will find a Ouija board story that follows a mysterious encounter in a mine in Norway:

"The Haunted Mine"

Transcription Assisted & Edited
by Birke Duncan

3:00 p.m., January 22, 1999. Birke Raymond Duncan was born in Bellevue, Washington April 10, 1967. He lived on Bainbridge Island (1977-1994), Seattle (1995-1996) and later resided in Poulsbo. Birke completed his B.A. in English Language and Literature at the University of Washington in 1989. Subsequently, Birke achieved an M.A. in Scandinavian Folklore and Mythology at the UW in 1997. He then occupied himself with folklore studies and what he called, "office drudgery."

This memorate and family legend were told in the same session when Ben, one of our informants, told his various tales. One legend leads to another in a communal setting; this mini-legend-telling session was proof of that. All of us mentioned something regarding the supernatural at one point or another. Birke in fact began his tale first before we questioned Ben:

"In 1991, I attended the International Summer School at the University of Oslo. I was one of sixty students and two professors who went on a five day bus trip from Oslo to Bergen and back. On the last leg of our trip, we had dinner in a rustic setting. It looked like a Viking longhouse with all these picnic tables inside. It was a farmyard in a place called Blaafarveverket, which means 'the blue color works' [referring to a glass blowing facility and cobalt mine.]

"Here we were in the middle of Norway, and what do you think they served us? Chili. I couldn't believe it. The guy sitting across from me was Andrew Brinkman. He was from Texas. He said something like, 'Oh boy, chili! They knew I was coming.' He couldn't wait to dig in. I just ate dinner rolls. I hate chili.

"There were sugar cubes in bowls in the middle of the table. Andrew said, 'You see these? I'm going to feed a sugar cube to one of those goats out there.'

"I said, 'You can't do that. It says in Norwegian, English, and German you're not supposed to feed the animals.'

"'Oh, yeah? Watch me.'

"After dinner, we went out. He climbed over a two-rail fence, and walked around the corner of the shed. Then he came running back out, climbed back over the fence, and said: 'That goat was evil. It wanted to kill me.' He looked around and said, 'Hey, look at that cave over there. Let's explore it.'

"I said, 'We can't do that. We'll get lost. You got lost in that castle in Bergen.'

"He said, 'C'mon.'

"Anyway, we went into this cave which was really an old cobalt mine, but we didn't know that. We walked in. He looked to the left and said, 'Hi, how are you?' Then he yelled: 'Eee-yaaah! There's a human head in there.'

"I looked, and there was. I went like this: 'Eeee-ye-uhhhh!' [Birke shudders in a protracted expression of fright.]"

Ben asked, "A skeletal head, or flesh?"

Birke replied, "It was more flesh. It had sunken cheeks, purple skin, no eyes–just holes where the eyes should have been–and disheveled brown hair. I looked back–and it was gone."

"Are you serious?" asked Ben.

Birke said, "I hope it was a trick of the light which we both saw."

"So you both saw it?"

"Yes, we both saw it," said Birke, "I even questioned him the next day. I said, 'Were you putting me on? Was there really something in there?'

"He said, 'Yeah!'

"I couldn't believe it at the time. He's in the Air Force now." Birke looked at the tape recorder: "Is this thing still on? Bugging my conversation? You'll transcribe that on our own."

After some prodding, Birke had another story as well, and it was the first one in which the infamous Ouija board plays a role.

286

Birke said, "This was supposed to be about him [Ben]. Hmm…My Aunt Roberta had this friend named Connie who was married to a guy named Tom Swinlund. He was a practical joker, which is very important to this story. They were on a trip in Italy. They [Connie and Tom] went out onto a kind of parapet or something where you could look at the ocean. Tom said, 'Hey, Connie, look at me.' He jumped off the edge. This was his idea of a practical joke. Unfortunately, he thought he was jumping onto solid ground. It [a ledge] broke away[Tom fell], and he got killed."

Jason Harris commented, "That's horrible."

"Yes, it is," said Birke. "A year or two later–I don't know what the time frame is–Connie was visiting my Aunt Roberta. They pulled out a Ouija board to play with it. They were looking for a presence and they found one:

"'Can you tell us who you are?'

"'Yes.'

"'What is your name?'

"'It spelled out 'T-O-M-S-W-I-N-L-U-N-D: his name. Well, that spooked the living daylights out of them, so they put the board away. They never played with it again."

Jason asked, "That was kind of hasty, don't you think?"

"Well," said Birke, "it was probably [Tom's] practical joke from beyond the grave."

"It could also be subconscious," said Jason.

"That's probably the most likely, but it doesn't make as good a story."

At this point, we moved on to Ben's experiences. For comparative purposes however, here is Andrew Brinkman's account of the haunted mine. Andrew sent his email response all the way from Germany:

"Here is my story and I'm sticking to it: On a fine summer day in sunny Norway back in 1991, I was walking along a wooded path along a series of cliffs in western Norway with my cohort in crime, and fellow time traveler, Master Birke R. Duncan, a.k.a. 'Dark Lord of the Forest.'

We were on a field trip from our International Summer School (ISS) Oslo classes and [...] somehow our discussions turned from WWII topics to queries about what might be inside some of the various cave entrances we were seeing on the face of the cliffs.

"We pondered episodes of *Gilligan's Island* featuring giant spiders inside caves, quickly ruled out pirate and Viking treasures, and even dismissed thoughts of residue from secret girl scout meetings. When we gained the courage to enter the cave (and believe me, as an Officer in the United States Air Force, I don't scare easily...now. Of course back then seeing a test of the Emergency Broadcast System on TV was enough to send me crying into the next room [...]. But I digress.). We both did so, cautiously. Allowing our eyes to adjust to the darkness, we were both amazed at what we saw...exiting the cave it was soon apparent that we had both seen what we believed to be a human head lying on the floor of the cave, leaning ever so gently against the cave wall. Can it be called "Mass" Hysteria if only two people saw something in the darkness? What demonic force willed us to see a human head? Or was there a human head in the cave that day?"

Andrew D. Brinkman, Capt. USAF, Spangdahlem Air Base, Germany.

Andrew retired from the Air Force as a Major in 2013. He also served in Korea, Romania, Bosnia, Croatia, and Afghanistan, among places. He then worked as Event Coordinator at the George C. Marshall Center for Security Studies in Germany.

"Ben & the Ouija Board"

by Ben Nguyen

The interview was part of the same session on January 22, 1999, at 3:00 p.m. Ben Nguyen was born on July 20, 1973 in Saigon, Vietnam. His grandfather was a general in the war against France, and his father worked for the CIA during the civil war. The family fled their country in 1975, and came to Seattle. Ben earned a B.A. in Political Science in 1998 and, at the time of our interview, worked as an office assistant for Custom Foods, part of the Uwajimaya grocery store chain. He was also in the process of applying for a US government job, which would continue his family tradition of national service. He also had extensive martial arts training. Ben had never related the story to anyone other than the people mentioned therein, until a conversation with my colleague.

Jason Marc Harris had spoken of his own interest in folklore, particularly ghost stories. He asked Ben if he had any experiences. It led to narration of a cycle of strange first and secondhand accounts:

"Tread Not on My Grave"

by Ben Nguyen

Ben told the story: "One day, all of us: Ti, Robin who owned the [Ouija] board, my older brother who shared the room with me, and I went to the graveyard on Delridge Way. I was surprised that the [Lakeview] cemetery was still open at one in the morning, and we could just go in. We got out the board. I was sure it was going to work; there had to be a lot of spirits around here. The pointer itself had trouble moving around. Maybe there were a lot of spirits trying to get it: 'I want a piece of it. I want a piece of it.'

"Maybe that's why it couldn't move right. It was just shaking. We spent the next twenty minutes trying to get a message out of it, but we got tired. Before we left, Robin had to go to the bathroom. He urinated, over by a tree somewhere in the distance. He came back, and we left.

"He next morning, he told me his mother asked him: 'Did you go to a graveyard last night?'

"'Yeah.'

"Robin's mother said, 'I had a dream last night of an old man. He told me not to let my son and his friends come to his territory and desecrate it.'

"Violent Urges From Beyond?"

Ben then narrated a secondhand tale about his brother Ti and friend Quoc who "pretty much lived with us rent free." After using the Ouija board, Quoc felt motivated in a dream to attack Ti.

292

Quoc refrained from doing so, and confessed to Ti of his violent urges.

Ti reassured Quoc it was just a nightmare.

Ben told us that then, mysteriously, "while they were talking, the Halogen lamp was turned on halfway. Suddenly, it just went off. Quoc reached over and turned it back on. Somehow the switch turned off by itself.

"That night, before they went to sleep, Quoc said my brother was keeping an eye on him. He had one eye open. After that, nobody played with the board anymore."

However, Quoc's brother Bau did use the board. This gave Bau's wife a dream that allegedly inspired her to try to kill Bau while she was sleeping. The "state of possession" ended when Bau woke his wife up. Unfortunately, Bau was now afraid of his wife.

"From that day on, he [Bau] vowed not to sleep with his wife until things got settled. To remedy this, he slept in the Buddhist temple. I did, too, because I still couldn't sleep for some reason.

"Ti wanted to get this monkey off his back, too.

"The monks gave us these Buddhist chant tapes. When I would play it at night, I could sleep easier. I could sleep like a baby. I wouldn't wake up at all.

"In the meantime, Bau used the temple as his place to rest. He couldn't sleep at home. He was scared of his wife. Everything's okay with them now: ever since they stopped playing with the [Ouija] board and started listening to the tapes.

"We asked the monks where these spirits were coming from.

"They [the monks] said: 'They're coming because the monastery holds the ashes of people who've been cremated.'

"We have a three-foot high Buddha statue facing our house. The spirits that did not make it into Heaven are repelled by Buddha's face. Our house is right across the street.

"The monks said, 'You've got to shut your windows to keep them out. An open window is an invitation for a spirit running away from the face of Buddha.'"

Epilogue by Birke Duncan

Jason Harris said, "That board brought a lot of chaos to a lot of people."

Ben said, "Yes."

My colleague's comment and Ben's response function as the coda, the final statement that wraps up the tale. This is appropriate, since Jason discovered the tale and encouraged its performance. The Buddhist faith has adapted to the times by putting their chants on tape. Tradition and technology ward off evil.

Ghosts of Relatives

Ghosts of relatives proved to be the most common manifestation among our informants' spiritual experience. The first example comes from Ben. It's a tale he told me on the first occasion when I heard his Ouija board stories. Birke was not present at this earlier session.

"Ghostly Inheritance"

by Ben Nguyen

[Jason begins:] "Let's just hear about some ghost stuff."

"Let's talk about my grandfather," said Ben. "When he died, they were trying to find the money that he said that he left. And they couldn't find it that night. And they all gave up [my Aunt, my Mom, and my Dad].

"The next day in the morning, my Mom said she had a dream of my grandfather. And he came back in the clothes that he died in, and he told where the money was kept.

"And she went frantically–woke up–checked underneath the wardrobe and there was the money taped underneath. It's weird about Asian families. It happens to them, but when I ask my friends of other races, it doesn't."

Notably in this interview when Ben told me his Ouija board tales, he remarked upon his initial fascination.

"I kept playing over and over again like that movie, *The Exorcist*."

Also, when we first discussed the Ouija board and I suggested that the subconscious plays a large role, before beginning his narrative, Ben asserted, "I'll prove you wrong right here."

In a later conversation, Ben told me about a night terror or incubus experience as well; it was standard fare–with difficulty moving and the presence sitting on the bed. Ben awoke and drove the hallucination, or spirit, away.

"Ghosts from Down Under"

by Rachel

I stumbled upon a group of people on my way back from the market one day and, after some conversation, inquired about ghostly lore. The result was the following tale by Rachel [alias]. She was from Australia–a friend of Amy [alias], a UW college student, and John was a homeless person camped near Amy's apartment. The two women were drunk.

Rachel: I was about seven years old. My brother is about three years younger than me. He was sleeping in the same bed. We were staying at my Nannie's [Australian term for grandmother] house.

So we were lying there and the door was open. And from that point on I could not sleep with my door closed. And this woman came around from the corner. She stood in the doorway. And I saw her. And my brother saw her, too, but his reaction was a little slower than mine. I thought it was my grandmother at first. But it wasn't, because she [the unknown woman] was about four feet off the ground.

Jason: The woman's feet were?

Rachel: Yeah. No. No, there were no feet. Her gown was like four feet off the ground. And she had a glow around her, so I knew something was strange. [She was] wearing a flowing cape dress [...]a hood on it [...] looked like a nightgown. Anyway, she was standing there. She had long blonde hair. My brother sat up [...] seemed like forever [...] sat up and stared at her. [He felt] like screaming but you couldn't hear it. All of a sudden I felt good. I'm totally protective of my brother. I walked out into the hallway. She was back a little ways [...] just four feet off the ground. Just floating. It was awesome. And I saw her. And I turned around like this and my Nannie – my grandmother–was standing at the doorway of her bedroom–which was right there–and she went like this, like covered her mouth.

Jason: Oh, so your grandmother saw her. What did your Grandma say about it? Just hug you and go back to bed?

Rachel: No hugs. That's not the way we're [we are] here. Just went back to bed. It parallels the way it is now: my relationship with my parents.

Jason: Oh really? In what way?

Rachel: Just...

Jason: You don't want to get into that.

Rachel: No.

It might have been interesting to plumb the depths of the relation between the family dynamics and the ghostly visitations, but Rachel firmly determined the parameters of the interview.

"Grandpa's Visit"

by Chris Aynesworth

Christopher Levin Aynesworth was born on April 18, 1973, in the Alta Bates Hospital in Berkeley, California. He spent his first seven years in Kensington, California, and was subsequently raised in Orinda. Chris graduated from the University of California at Santa Barbara with a degree in Sociology. He currently designs websites, but plans to make a living as an acoustic and electric guitarist.

Jason Harris interviewed Chris Aynesworth on March 25, 1999:

"I must have been seven," said Chris, "My Grandpa used to live in Fresno, and I went to go see him for Easter. The whole family went, and we brought our cocker spaniel, Bo. We had a good time there, and as we were leaving, we brought our cocker spaniel and put him in the car. I remember we were saying our good-byes. It was a really sunny day out. I was standing on his lawn. In Fresno, the lawns are all the same. Everyone is given the same little lawn in front of the house.

"Grandma kissed me on the head. Grandpa patted me on the head and said, 'Bye, boy.'

"I even remember holding a micronaut. Remember micronauts?"

They were action figures that kids could bend into multiple positions.

"The reason I remember it so clearly," Chris continued, "is because I felt it was a memorable event. It seemed special for some reason. A lot of things happened that day. We drove back home. It took us around two hours. When we got home, my Dad got a call that something had happened. I remember him running back to the car. And I said [child-like voice]: 'Aren't you going to read us a story?'

"I was very young, but I felt that something very bad had happened. I would learn, later on, that my

Grandpa had died. I stayed for about a week at a friend's house in El Cerrito after that.

"You see, since we brought the cocker spaniel, we took along this little gate that would keep the dog in the kitchen, so he wouldn't be wandering all over the house when everyone was asleep. We had accidentally left the gate behind. For some reason, my Grandfather thought he could catch up with us on the freeway, and give the dog gate to us. He packed it in the back of his car, tried to catch up to us. I guess it was very important for him to do that. And it seems now like an irrational, strange thing. Who would do that? We had left a half-hour earlier. Half an hour on the freeway is like thirty miles. In order to catch up to someone, you'd have to go almost twice as fast; so it doesn't make any sense."

Jason asked, "You didn't really need the dog gate, did you?"

"No, no, I mean we could always buy another one. They weren't that expensive. Anyway, my Grandfather had a heart attack on the freeway, while he was driving.

But somehow, he was able to control himself enough to go off to the side of the road. I always pictured him in this field; and he apparently just died. Just like that: in the car."

"He didn't crash?" asked Jason.

"No, he didn't crash. So, anyway: That was Easter morning.

"One year later, I remember saying good night to my parents. It was the night before Easter. I remember going to sleep. I woke up once because I felt kind of scared. It just kind of hit me: Grandpa died a year ago. I tried to sleep, but I couldn't. And then, there was no sound, but my eyes were closed.

"It was like someone flashed a camera in front of my eyes. And I could see the flash with my eyes closed. I opened my eyes and there was this figure standing in front of my bed. It was kind of swaying, like a subtle breeze was moving it. It was shaped in the silhouette of a human. It looked like it was composed of TV snow. I could see my night light through the figure.

"It was very scary. I knew it was my Grandpa. I didn't feel any sense of something evil, but there was a ghost. I knew I was seeing it. It wasn't really doing anything. I probably looked at it less than ten seconds, then burrowed into my blankets, and made myself into a ball at the foot of my bed. I didn't know what to do.

"I've told you this before–there was a cave made up of blankets. I slowly saw this hand come down through the sheets, and he did an up and down motion with his hand. I knew that he was trying to do the very thing that he last did to me, which was to pat me on the head.

"I couldn't scream, but finally I forced myself to scream [strained, strangled cry:] 'Dad!'

"My Dad was probably like twenty feet away. When I heard my Dad getting up and stomping around, the same thing happened. There was a flash. I don't know if my eyes were closed or not, but I didn't see him come and I didn't see him go. I was afraid to open my covers.

"I told my Dad. He seemed interested, but as if I were telling him a philosophical concept. He said, 'Oh, that's interesting.'

"Sometimes when I really want things to go my way, I'll say, 'Grandpa, help me.' We have the same initials. He was Charles Levin Aynesworth. I'm Chris Levin Aynesworth. He was a traveling jazz performer." Chris is a guitarist, so they have musical talent in common.

"I didn't tell anyone else," said Chris, "like my brother or my Mom, for two years. I remember I told my best friend at the time, Stephan. I drew a picture of it."

"Chris's Ouija Board"

by Chris Aynesworth

Chris first narrated how he used a Ouija board in the dormitory at UC-Santa Barbara, where I also lived at the time. Mysterious phenomena allegedly followed: a door uncannily opened three times in a row, and an invisible visitor rapped on the door in three bursts in a row. The following memorat, however, is particularly interesting because in this case Chris Levin Aynesworth believed he experienced effects of a Ouija board session in which he was not a participant.

Chris narrated: "I had dropped in on Jinn's [alias]room, and he was playing with a Ouija board by himself. About a half-hour later, I was doing something in my room and I was thirsty. I got my cup and wanted to get some really cold water. I went out to the drinking fountain by the elevator, filled my cup, and walked back the other way. You know how the singles' hall was. It was closed off with two glass doors. One was closer to your room, and my room.

"Within about fifteen feet of the door, I had the back of my hair stand up. And that happened first. And I felt: 'There's something there.' I didn't want to turn around. I looked to see what was in the reflection of the glass, but I didn't see anything. I sped up and opened the door, and I was like: 'ooo-oh-oh [shudder]!' I have some of these chills sometimes when I'm scared.

"I went into my room really fast, and I turned around as the door was closing. There was a foot of door space as it closed, and I saw this big, black shape move. It didn't bounce up and down like it had legs. It was more like a big barrel with something on top of it, like a head. But by then, the door had closed so I didn't get to see much of it. I saw it for maybe half a second."

Jason said, "You probably didn't want to look at it, either."

"No," said Chris. "That really scared me. I wonder now, why didn't it just go into my room?"

Five seconds of silence followed the question.

Chris continued: "Five or ten minutes later, I knocked on Jinn's door and told him about it: 'This weird thing happened to me.'

"He was all [gasp]: 'Really?' He was surprised. He had asked not too long ago for something [a "demon] to appear and scare the hell out of me. He thought it was funny. I didn't like that he had asked for that. It had worked. That proves that something had happened. I didn't know what he was doing. You can't pretend that there's something behind you, and have a natural reaction."

This ends Birke's transcription.

Epilogue by Jason Marc Harris

Chris went on to tell about seeing a shadowy form in his house when he was about eleven years old: "Part of the shadow had sort of a Robin Hood cap on it. I could see its arms, and it had balled its fists like to run. Thinking about it now, maybe it was like a gnome or a little forest creature."

Place Legends, "Fairies of the Field"
&
"The Ghost of Dunsany Castle"

by Samuel Barton

Samuel Barton [alias], Friday, June 25, 1999. Mr. Barton is a local playwright who has successfully written & produced for the stage, TV, and film. His French father "was a warlock." His mother was Russian, and a performing dancer.

"I have a great belief in things such as the 'little people,' said Samuel Barton, 'In the early [nineteen]seventies I was invited to bring one of my theatrical productions to Dundalk [County Louth, Ireland], which is just to the south of Belfast, a quaint little town. I became friendly with the staff where the company stayed, and one of the waitresses there said, 'Would you like to experience something very unusual?'

"And I said, 'Sure, why not?'

"So, we went out driving and we came to an area in the country where there is a slope in the road, a kind of deep depression in the road, and his young lady–whose name I've long since forgotten–drove the car to the bottom of this slope. Then she took her feet off the gas and her hands off the driving wheel, and the car rose back [pause] up to the top of this grade [pause for drama again], all by itself.

"She said, 'Look around. Do you see those tiny little trees?'

309

"And they were kind of like–I don't know if you are familiar with manzanita trees. They have many, many little gnarls, like little apple trees." His voice pattern changed for this digression. One can clearly hear the temporary suspension of the core narrative on tape, by the voice tone.

Jason said, "They have red bark."

"Yes, that's right," said Samuel Barton, "charming little trees. And they were in fields that had been completely plowed around them. They were called 'fairy trees' and fairies are supposed to live either in or at the base of these trees; and they were many, many, many surrounding this area and I was: 'aaahhhhh' [gasp]!"

Jason said, "I thought it was some kind of Thorn. So there are different trees sacred to fairies then. Thorn and Manzanita?"

Samuel replied, "I think Manzanita is a tree that looks similar to these. They're very, very–you've seen apple trees— and they're deliberately dwarfed, and they're gnarled, and they're enchanting things, and they look like fairy tale trees. Another experience I also had [emphasis:] in Ireland."

"Did I interrupt that one?" asked Jason.

"That was really the end. My mouth hung open for days. She pointed out the trees and said this was an extremely potent area for fairy activity. Especially at the new moon rather than the full moon [...]. She said there's a lot of activity that goes on [...] a lot of disturbance in the area; a lot of pranks that are played; and I believe in that."

Jason said, "So this was one of the pranks."

"Some kind of energy that existed; some kind of strange energy. This was a long time ago. This was in the [nineteen]seventies [...]. I went again to Ireland on another project to make a motion picture which was earlier than that [the fairy story]. It was a musical version of *The Prince and the Pauper* and we stayed at a place called Castle Dunsany. Are you familiar with that?"

"Lord Dunsany?"

"Lord Dunsany's castle. Yes...a very, very [like many, many]weird things happened. I was given a wonderful chamber in which to sleep, and I went to bed. And I got up about two o'clock in the morning. I went to bed around twelve–I'm not sure–I was asleep for about two hours. And the door to the room was wide open. I got up, closed the door, and went back to sleep, and [soon] I was up [again] and the light was coming through the hallway. The door: it was wide open again!

"I sat and thought for a while. I decided I would put a chair underneath, to keep the door closed. I did that and went back to sleep. And I was awakened again, and the door was wide open, and the chair was right back where I had taken it from, to place it."

Jason said, "And you found that odd?"

"Well now," explained Samuel, "I was getting creeped. There was a kind of sideboard close to the door, and a heavy marble-top arrangement–very ornately carved–and I pulled that in front of the door, and I watched for about fifteen minutes. And I just watched, and watched, and watched, and finally I drifted off.

"And I woke up the next morning. The door was wide open. And the piece–which made a lot of noise when it moved across the floor–"

Jason inserted, "When you moved it."

"When I moved it," Samuel continued, "It was right back in place and there were no marks on the floor other than the ones I might have made when I moved it. And I asked, I asked about the castle if it might be haunted. And the steward, that is our equivalent of butler, said, 'Oh, absolutely, oh yes, for hundreds of years.'"

"Was there any legend; how it started?" asked Jason.

"I don't remember a legend. I do remember–we filmed in the library of the castle an enormous affair, a huge stone fireplace at one end, and the butler reached–to show us a little trick of the castle–reached and pulled what appeared to be the flue-chain, and the whole fireplace swung. The hearth and everything just swung open. And it was now the wine cellar, but it used to be the torture chamber. I loved it, I loved it, I loved it!"

Mr. Barton ended the session by asking about my career plans–a decisive shift in topic. The storytelling was over.

"Haunted Apartments"

by Gordon Dwyer

11:15, on Saturday January 30, 1999. Believe it or not, a ghost story can lead to legal troubles. An apartment manager in Seattle told us that his building's owner might accuse him of interfering with the rental of her property if he divulged the place's secrets. As such, we have changed several names in the text.

Gordon Dwyer [alias] is the son of Irish immigrants. Ghost stories are hardly new to him, since his mother maintains a repertoire of banshee lore. However, not all traditions survived intact. The family converted from Catholicism to Lutheranism shortly after their arrival in America. Our informant's mother has displayed her Protestantism by wearing orange, instead of green, on St.

Patrick's Day. Orangemen are the Scots-Irish Protestants of Northern Ireland.

Gordon was born on March 6, 1959, in Seattle. He moved to the Larch [alias] Apartments in 1979 [in the University District], and later became the manager. The building is squat, three stories tall, with concrete walkways. The cramped accommodations are dimly lit and drafty. We sat on metal folding chairs that froze our legs.

The building also has a strange past in terms of rumor and legend. On three different occasions, women with no history of mental illness [allegedly], heard commands from demonic voices.

Preface, Part II
by Jason Marc Harris

I talked to the renter in number eleven, and he described hearing voices, having a Buddhist exorcism, and later hearing that in the apartment next to him, a woman tried to kill herself. However, he did not want to be interviewed even under an alias. Lacking his testimony the narrative lacks intensity, thus we now present Gordon's experience in:

"The Haunted Hotel"

by Gordon Dwyer

"Oh, yeah, the Meany Tower," said Gordon, "That's a really old hotel overlooking Forty-Fifth [Street] and Brooklyn [Ave.] opened in 1931. One day, I went up to do some work– moving stuff from one side of the room to the other. There were no lights up there, except for my flashlight. It sounded like a dinner party was going on. I heard my name called really loud: 'Gordon, why don't you jump?'

"I ran out of there so fast. The people who worked there used to tell me quite a bit of stories that went on. There were quite a few suicides there in the thirties, during the Depression. It used to be a flophouse. You could stay there for a couple bucks. You could wash your clothes, have a meal, and move on. It wasn't really luxurious. They used to have people jump out of the windows who were broke, had no job, no hope, and no future.

"In their main ballroom, there's quite a bit of activity. Back in the thirties, they used to have elegant cotillions and balls. They just recently turned it back into a ballroom, exactly the way it was. [There is a] big mirror. You can look in the mirror and see someone following behind you; you look around, and they're gone. All of the staff members told me about that, but I never saw anyone in it. For about fifty or sixty years, it was a lunch cafeteria, and just recently they renovated it back into a ballroom. There's one place where you can go outside and walk all the way around the penthouse. You get a really strong urge to jump.

"My supervisor, Erik, and I were up there, and we went outside. He was a chain smoker, so he had to go up there all the time. I told him about it, and he said, 'Oh, yeah, we all get that strong suicidal tendency.'

"He stopped going up there and went to smoke out back instead, because something's telling him to jump."

"The Shadow That Should Not Be"

by Gordon Dwyer

Gordon had mentioned this experience during conversation, so I decided to record it.

"It was a week ago, on Sunday night at ten p.m. I noticed this shadow, this hooded dark figure, casting a shadow on the kitchen cabinets moving right into the room. As soon as he went into the living room, he disappeared.

"It gave me the creeps. I kept the light on all night. There was nothing to cast a shadow. It's probably related to some of the stuff [hauntings] I've heard in the apartments."

"A Murdered Man's Revenant in a House"

by Dan Parr

Dan Parr is a married man in his forties, a skilled carpenter, and building specialist. He grew up in Seattle. He began his family legend with little prompting:

"The family immigrated here from Minneapolis in 1933 and the story is they [...] rented a house near Seattle Center. I think it was Sixth Avenue [North], two story house [...], late [nineteen-] thirties [...]. It wasn't the early forties yet. Two teenage sons that she had, and her was [sic] in the house."

On the mysterious occasion, "they looked up, and there at the front entrance of the house, there was a man standing there–a stranger; somebody they had never seen before. And he stood and looked at them for a moment, and he turned and walked up the stairs that were right there at the entry door. They [the mother and sons] heard his footsteps.

"They [the footsteps] walked down the middle of the hall, and stopped right around the middle of the bathroom.

"The two teenage boys ran up the stairs, following him, and when they got up the stairs, there was no one there.

"Now, there was also a back stairway from the upstairs that went out the backside of the house and they assumed he must have made it down there, and took off.

"Well, sometime later their youngest daughter was in high school[in] Queen Anne talking to people. She told them [the two brothers] that she had heard that a murder had been committed in the house. There was a man that was killed; his body had been cut up, and was hidden in a hot water tank, which was right outside the bathroom, where the footsteps had stopped."

Jason asked, "Boy, so they figured that was the victim or the murderer?" He and Dan laugh.

"Oh, I would say the victim," said Dan. I don't know what happened to the murderer [...] if he was caught

[...] don't know anything more about that story than that. But I heard that story several times from my grandmother."

Jason said, "Then the sister in the story heard about this story from another source?"

"Right, the background."

"That's interesting," Jason then asked, "How many times did your grandmother tell this?"

Dan replied, "Oh, several times and it was told similarly enough each time that I feel there is a certain amount of credibility there [pause] which wasn't always the case with my Grandmother."

Epilogue by Jason Harris

I asked Dan about his beliefs.

He said neither he nor his grandmother was a "believer" but that personal experience had affected both of them: "As a kid I remember having chills run up and down my back, because it was coming from someone I knew, so I had to give it some credibility."

Dan also went on to tell about a coworker who claimed to have out-of-body experiences and encountered beings from other dimensions. This was too "wild" for Dan to believe. He had also heard "The Hook" legend.

Raindancer Cafe Interviews
Transcribed by
Jason Marc Harris

The following transcriptions are all from employees of the Raindancer Cafe, and I list them together to show partly how one informant may lead to another, so to speak. The majority of the cases below involve haunted houses, which continues the theme of "place legends." We also have a highly unusual tale of the doppelganger.

"It Had My Heart Pumping at the Time" by Steve Clemens

Steve Clemens is the co-owner of the Raindancer Cafe, he is a talented chef and a poised speaker:

"So, anyhow, the story is: I've got a story. It might seem anti-climactic because I didn't actually see anything with my eyes, but it had my heart pumping at the time.

322

"The way it works out is I'd been away in New York for a couple of years, and my mother had moved into a new house. She started telling me these stories about weird things that had been going on since they'd moved in.

"Initially there was a groundskeeper, and he believed the house was haunted. And he relayed this one story: He heard some voices that were upset, and then a big crash as though a glass had been thrown against a brick wall. [The groundskeeper] came running out, got his shotgun, came running out of the room, and when we got into the area, there was no glass–no nothing.

"Yet there was water dripping down the chimney. That clued my mother in [that something mysterious was afoot.]

"When she started living there, it was the blue room that she thought was haunted: voices laughing as though they were at an old dance or something [from] the eighteen hundreds. She actually said it [sounded like] an old phonograph [gramophone] with the big horn. She and my sister actually heard this music. They could hear it coming out of the blue room. But when they entered, nothing happened.

"When they first moved in, a repairman had been up sleeping in the blue room, who said the clock was off at one-ten every night [...] three nights in a row. I thought this was great, I was going to stay in the blue room with all the ghosts, and check it out, because I'm a non-believer."

"So you were curious," Jason observed.

"Exactly. The first night I lay down, really hoping for something to happen."

"Did the clock quit running?"

"You know, it did. Right around the same time. Everything jibed. I remember thinking there was no ghost. The next day, I don't think anything happened. I'd blown it off. But on the third night: I can hear something like breathing coming from the foot of the bed.

"So, I sat there and said, 'The window's open,' and thought: 'It must be cars.'

"Then I said, 'No, it's coming from the base of the bed.'

"And then I thought, "No, this is too inconsistent. If it were cars from the highway, it would be sporadic; it wouldn't be consistent in and out breathing.

"At this point, I think, 'S—! It is coming from the base of the bed. There's something there. Something's going on.'

"So, sure enough, I summoned up all my courage, and my heart was really pumping... [looked] and saw absolutely nothing.

"And then I kicked back, and my heart was really pumping, and I tried listening for the breathing again but I heard nothing [...]. It really had me going at the time."

Jason said, "Well, seeing doesn't have to be believing; hearing can be believing, too."

"I totally agree," Steve replied.

"Maybe something happened at one-ten in the morning, in some history?"

"My mother did a little research," said Steven, "but that house had only been built in the nineteen-fifties. You'd have to go back a lot further than she did, by talking around."

Jason asked, "Did you tell your mother about this?"

"Oh, of course, and they said, 'What did we tell you?' The next day I was saying, 'I'm a believer' and told that story one hundred times in a week, because it was so fresh. This was actually ten or eleven years ago [1988 or 1989], and I hadn't really thought about it, till talking to you."

"So, it wore off after a while?"

"Yeah, you know, after not seeing a ghost every night. With time, you have to question things but at the time, you couldn't convince me other than that there was something there."

"Does it affect your worldview at all?" asked Jason.

"Just one of those things you file away as unexplained."

The conversation about ghostly matters led Steve Clemens to then tell a tale about an out-of-body experience.

"I had this girlfriend," said Steve, "She was a very credible person; very good mental health I would say. She relayed this one story to me how her boyfriend had developed a very large tumor, the size of a baseball in his head. He was on the verge of dying. [The boyfriend claimed] that during the operation, he left his body and was hovering over his body and was looking down at the doctors' operation [...] came back [to] his body [...and] recovered. [Later he] was living with my old girlfriend. And I guess from the very get-go, he claimed he could leave his body."

Jason said, "So, the first time he was able to learn, was in the hospital."

"Yeah," said Steve, "She woke up one night and saw him [astral body] hovering over them in bed. He

327

[physical body] was in bed next to her. She gets mad and tells him to get back in his body."

After they broke up for non-spiritual reasons, "She didn't tell him where she moved to. He had never been to her place before. He did have her phone number. He called her one night, and happened to tell her he visited her last night. He goes, 'Believe me, you have a nice place.'

"He started describing how she arranged her furniture and everything. She thought it was so bizarre, because he had been there.

"He said, 'I just want to be there, and I'm there.'"

Jason asked Steve Clemens about his spiritual beliefs.

Steven explained, "I was brought up to believe nothing in particular, as far as my upbringing. I went a handful of times as far as church-related activities. So after that it was just experiences: what you see on televisions, movies, and talking to people. I believe I have an open mind about it and definitely take the stance, 'I'll believe it when I see it."

Epilogue by Jason Harris

I then questioned Steve about whether his mother believed in ghosts, and he asserted that everybody did, and then said to me, "Do you believe in ghosts?"

I replied that it was "a big universe" and hearing so many tales of ghosts kept my mind open.

Steven then asked an employee, Marta, a young woman in her twenties, whether she had any ghost tales. And she did, as you may see below.

"Miscellaneous Hauntings and a Doppelganger."

by Marta Montgomery and Kerie Frisinger

Marta Montgomery, a woman in her twenties, worked as a bartender at the Raindancer.

Jason Harris said, "So, you have a few ghost stories."

Marta told Jason of how she moved into a house while in high school: "The radio would come on [mysteriously]; the TV set would come on. We'll start with my young brother [Brady]. His experience was

329

standing in the kitchen one day, and he was making Top Ramen. One of his best friends was over. The house was huge–really old house–[and there was] some old crockery inside of the house.

"And John [alias] came along into the kitchen–he saw him walk in, and asked, 'What are you making?'

"Brady says, 'I just told you: Top Ramen, and you didn't want any.'

"Brady turns around, and there's no one there.

"He [Brady] thought he [John] must have walked out of the room, or whatever. He finishes up, and starts to leave, and sees John again.

"So Brady is walking behind him, and they get to a doorway, where they're going to turn down a long hallway. And he [John] stops right in front of him [Brady], and you can't see through this person at all. And Brady was like: 'Move, John. Go.'

"And he was just standing there, and Brady went to push him.

"And his hand went right through, and it [the image of John] was gone. There was nothing there.

"And [the real] John was right there, [farther] down the hallway, going, 'What are you doing?'"

Jason remarked to Marta, "Usually that's supposed to be a bad omen." Namely, imminent death.

"Oh, really?" asked Marta. She laughed and said: "Then I walked through the house, just skipping through the house, and I wasn't thinking about anything. I went on to the hall light and–you know how you do a double-take? You kind of look where you're going to look, and you already know you're going to be looking ahead afterwards. So, I look, and there's a person standing in the living room. And it was just the perfect outline of a person, just standing there looking at you. Without any eyes. [The body was] just totally empty in the middle–the perfect outline of his friend [John], and you could see that [it] had [its] hands in some sort of pockets, just standing there."

Jason said, "So, the face was blank?"

331

"Blank," Marta confirmed. "Everything was blank in the interior. And so when I looked I had already turned my head and I saw it perfectly, like a full view of this, and I turned back and it was gone."

"You think that it was the same thing?" asked Jason. Was it the same as the earlier double of John?

"I think it was the same thing," said Marta.

She also explained seeing the outline of a person standing near the bed at night, that would then disappear. She had never heard of the doppelganger tradition, and didn't seem interested in hearing about it either. However, she did have a tale about poltergeist activity:

"In my house, I never felt anything really bad. I was never afraid [about the house], but in the backyard, I always had a bad feeling. More things happened [there in the yard, where they built a shed]. My boyfriend was staying with me in the shed [...]. We were asleep, and we were hearing footsteps around the shed, and [surprisingly] the dog [a Chow] was laying down. It wasn't barking.

"And then all of a sudden we heard knocking from underneath the floorboards, which are like paper thin. We're frozen because we're so terrified. Then I started hearing little kids. Kind of like that movie *Poltergeist*, where you have the verse of sounds that fluctuate from really light to strong voices, to really light again: like kids playing on the playground.

"So I'm saying, 'Am I going insane? Does this person [her boyfriend] hear this, too?'

"I'm hearing all these little kids playing, tether balls ringing, balls bouncing, and there's this really forced laughing. Not normal kids' laughter. It's really scary, and there's this prominent voice on top of it: 'Let me in.'

"The person I'm with says, 'Do you hear children, and balls bouncing, and tether balls?'

"And I say, 'Yes!'

"We're just terrified. We're looking out [the window], and there's nothing out there. We just can't take it anymore. We went to open the shed door, and something slammed boom right against it. You know the sheds are so loud–they're made out of aluminum–when something hits it. Like thunder.

"We finally just opened the door, and there was nothing. Completely quiet. No bad feeling either.

"I talked to my brother afterwards, and he had the same experience. I always had a really bad feeling about the backyard, like someone was watching you, but it's out in the middle of the desert–there's nobody there."

Marta explained this was in Indio, California, close to Palm Springs near a Reservation for The Cahuilla Nation.

Apparently her father also had mysterious experiences in the house. He experienced poltergeist activity, despite his skepticism, while watching *Silence of the Lambs*. Toy reindeer "flew thirteen or fourteen feet and landed in front of his feet."

Marta also revealed that some friends would spontaneously cry in the house. She also learned that the house had a history allegedly connected to violence: "Our

334

next door neighbor says the previous owner's son had killed himself in the house, but I don't know if that's true."

Marta claimed to have trouble with poltergeist activity in an apartment she used to live in, as well. The word "look" would mysteriously appear on the television, and the front door mysteriously locked in front of Marta and her roommate. She asserted she "always" has believed in ghosts.

After speaking with Marta, I met Kerrie Frisinger who works as a waitress at the Raindancer. She told about the "women's dormitory" at Ohio State "which was formerly an infirmary apparently, so it was haunted by people who had died in that infirmary."

She described poltergeist activity with her sister's clock, the fan, and an electronic door.

Kerrie also mentioned Belhurst Castle, a stone mansion in Geneva, New York, later converted into a hotel. It had a picture where people claimed the eyes would move: "It's a picture of a little boy who died in that house apparently. There are noises in the attic–typical things like that. They always tell people to go in there. They like to use it as part of the charm, basically. I don't know what the truth is."

Kerrie believes in ghosts, she says, because of her "belief in the afterlife" though "not necessarily" a "religious" afterlife. "I guess I believe in the soul lasting after a person dies. It might be just fear, a fear of the unknown."

Second Sight:
Precognition, Fetches, & Wraiths
"Visionary Family Reunions"

by Gail Duncan

The first informant presented here is Birke's mother, Gail Imogene Birkedahl Duncan. She is a second generation American. Her paternal and maternal grandparents came from Norway. Born in Grand Forks, North Dakota on February 8, 1937, she has lived in Portland, Oregon (1939-1959), California, and Wyoming before residing in Washington from 1962 to the time of this book's writing and repackaging.

Mrs. Duncan earned her B.S. degree in Social Sciences before she became a public school teacher. She is retired, and has been married to Gene Emerson Duncan since 1961.

The interview took place in Poulsbo on June 19, 1999, the same day as a barbecue Ashley Morris [Chapter 3, "Experiences with Fairies"] invited Birke and me to, where we would later record a legend-telling session around the campfire.

Jason said, "You had some vision, you were saying?"

Mrs. Duncan explained, "I had this neighbor, Mrs. Copeland, who was 81 years old, and she was ill with leukemia. I had talked to her in the hospital, and she was feeling quite well, like she was going to recover.

"I dreamed about her. Mrs. Copeland was in her front yard. Her cheeks looked pink, as if she'd had a blood transfusion. She was wearing an elegant pantsuit that was tweed. I had never seen it before. I told her how nice she looked. She said she felt really good.

"She died that night, unbeknownst to me.

"My husband and I went to her funeral a few days after that. We had to file past her open coffin. I looked down, and there she was with pink cheeks, looking exactly as she had in my dream complete with the pantsuit that I had never seen her wear. The exact same."

Jason asked, "Did you sort of gasp when you saw that?"

"I was quite taken aback."

Birke was a small child at the time. He later added, "I remember when my parents came home from the funeral. My mother looked dazed." That was the first time Mrs. Duncan told the story: right after it happened.

Mrs. Duncan continued telling her stories, on June 19, 1999: "I also saw my [deceased] Dad, but I saw him when I was awake. It was the day of his funeral [in May of 1986]. All the relatives were congregated on my mother's patio. And there was my Dad sitting there, leaning forward, and smiling at my brother-in-law [Lee Jones]. My brother-in-law had been cleaning gutters all day, and doing all kinds of nice things for my mother. And then he [Dad] just dissolved into his sister [Mandy]. It had been clearly him. He disappeared. It was really weird.

"I've sensed his presence a lot. I still do, but I've never seen him again."

Birke prompted: "Tell about what he said to you."

"I was worried about the car we were driving in, and everything. It was an old car, and in bad shape. He said it would be all right."

"You just heard his voice?" asked Jason.

"Yes," said Mrs. Duncan, "And I heard his voice the day of his funeral in the morning. He said, 'Well, anyway, it was a nice day.'"

We all laughed.

"Always optimistic," said Mrs. Duncan, "He always saw the better side of everything."

Jason asked, "What was the occasion of the car?"

"It was an old Ford station wagon, and the steering was bad. We had to get everybody in the car. The ruts were so bad that my husband was having a hard time keeping it on the road."

"This was on the way to the funeral?" Jason asked.

"Yes. It was really something I was concerned about. Our family was in it, so I didn't want anything to happen. He [her father] said it would be all right, and it was."

This is a case where the ghost allays anxiety.

Jason asked, "So did you believe in such things as ghosts before you had these sights?"

"I'm open to it," said Mrs. Duncan, "I don't disbelieve it at all, because it's really uncanny how I could feel my Dad. My sister could, too. I can sense that she [her sister Roberta of the Ouija board story] is going to call me. We do have a real connection. People used to think we were twins."

Jason asked, "Have any more of your family members seen anything?"

"My mother saw lots of things. She was an R.N. [Registered Nurse], so people were dying, and she had experiences.

"I know my [paternal] grandmother [Gena Westby Birkedahl Westland] saw her first husband [Pedar Birkedahl in the 1920s]. He had a halo of light around his head when he died."

"It sounds like he was going to the right place," said Jason.

"I think so. He was a cop, and an awfully nice guy."

Mrs. Duncan went on to talk about her father's family. There were no supernatural tales, just stories about homesteading in North Dakota. She suggested a possible reason for the lack of supernatural material; "They're [the family] a type of Christian–Lutheran–that it is almost sinful to believe in anything like that."

"A Fetch or Wraith
&
"A Murder Revealed in a Vision"

by Leanna

March 1999, Birke and I met Leanna by chance, as she played the piano in Hansee dormitory at the University of Washington. She studied English and Spanish.

Leanna said, "By coincidence, my family went on vacation to New Zealand, a month ago. And my grandmother called to tell us her brother died. We didn't know him that well. We were just visiting our great-grandmother a couple of weeks ago. We just walk in, and she's kind of senile, and she says, 'Oh, is that you, Leanna?'

"We walk in," [Leanna reasserted rhythm and focus through repetition of a phrase] and she said, 'Jimmy came to visit me'--which is her adopted son– 'And we had a conversation, and he was sort of crying. And he said, 'Well, you're not my real Mom.' But then we talked and he kind of left.'

"And we said, 'How long ago was this?'

"And she said, 'Two weeks', which is when he died.

"She's also not usually lucid enough to have a conversation. We just sort of looked at each other and said, 'That's really eerie.'

"We're not like a religious family. It really made me think. Could he really have come and visited her? So that really happened–a firsthand account."

Birke added, "And it's very common, too."

"I've heard that," Leanna agreed. "My Grandma, who is very academic, started talking about [Carl] Jung. I guess he recorded a lot of cases of stories like that. No one had told her [Leanna's great-grandmother] that her son had died. No one had called her."

Apparently, the family thought the great-grandmother wouldn't understand the situation, because of her senility.

I inquired about her beliefs. Leanna's father was raised Catholic. As for ghosts, Leanna said, "I don't know.

I wouldn't deny the possibility of things, but I also wouldn't go too far and say I understand this is how it happened–just because there are a lot of things we don't understand."

"Do you think it has changed your life; your point of view?"

Leanna said, "I guess if I heard people with similar stories I won't be as skeptical. Oh, another story my Mom used to tell me." Leanna laughed and said, "This is like in three sentences. I guess she knew this family that had two sons, and they both got into drugs. And one of them went missing–like a drug deal went bad. So they expected the worst, and the police couldn't find his body. And this cousin had a vision and they went to the place of where it was, and found him strangled. So now I guess I would be more susceptible to belief."

Note the tendency towards evaluative statements in her narratives, such as "I guess I would be more susceptible." Stylistically, "I guess" is a repeated tic, which emphasizes her introspective tendency. Another interesting stylistic feature is that Leanna uses "we" continuously in the first tale–signifying the communal aspect of the experience–while in the second tale, Leanna chooses to use "I" since it is a more individual experience: something her mother told only her, apparently. Examples of the communal stylistics of the first narrative include phrases such as "we're not a very religious family" and reference to her grandmother's allusion to Carl Jung– emphasizing that there was communal involvement in the evaluation of the legend.

"A Life of Second Sight"

by Denise

Interview on April 9, 1999. Denise works at the College Inn. Her very young daughter, Francesca, was with her at the interview. Birke let Francesca hold his index fingers while she toddled around the room.

Notably, Denise's relatives are from Scotland, a land known for second sight.

Denise said, "My Grandma knew things that there was no way she could have known. And in the family, there are lots of stories but [this is the one] that everybody knows.

"My Grandpa worked for the railroad. He worked the graveyard shift, and one night he got a telegraph that there had been a flash flood in the hills, on the far side of town, not the side where the river was. This was in Montana, during the Depression.

"And there had been a flash flood up on the Rimrock, on the other side of the river, and so the flood was coming. But it wasn't going to come from the river. It was going to come from the other side of town. And so he went to check on his family who lived on that side of town.

"And when he pulled up in the driveway at two o'clock in the morning, my Grandma had all four of the girls hauling water and putting it up in high places, and moving all the valuable things up high. He walked into the house, and he said, 'May, what are you doing?'

"And she said [slight vocal imitation:], 'Now, Obert, don't tell me I'm crazy, but I had a dream.' I guess that's what she called it. 'There was water in the house and it was going up to here.' And she marked a spot on the wall, and she said, 'I just know it's going to happen.'

"And he [Obert] was dumb. He was kind of dumbfounded because he had just gotten a telegraph. He was coming to tell her that, but she already visualized it. [great emphasis:] Water came into the house and it came exactly where she said it was going to come.'"

I then asked for other occasions of her grandmother's second sight.

Denise answered, "When she was like, eleven–I don't remember the exact details of it–her older sister disappeared. They hired private detectives. They finally hired a person who was a psychic. He came to the house.

"She [Denise's grandmother] was a kid and had been sent inside. She came running into the room. She stopped, and was just staring at him.

"And he [the psychic] said to her: 'Go on.'

347

"Her mother was saying, 'May, how rude of you to run in here and interrupt us grownups.'

"And he said–he looked right at her: 'Go on, May, tell her where you know me.'

"Somehow, they had some connection already. [May] had seen [the psychic] in a dream. And he told her [now]: 'You have a gift. You have second sight. Always trust it. It will never tell you anything wrong. Don't let other people talk you out of it, or ridicule you for it.'"

Denise added, "That, to me, is intriguing."

"Where was this?" I asked.

"It was Montana."

"So, she lived in Montana. So what happened? Did they find her [the missing sibling]?"

Denise paused before answering: "She was dead."

Birke looked up from the helping Francesca toddle. He asked, "Murdered?"

"Hmm?"

Birke inquired, "Was she murdered?"

Denise replied, "I think the husband, the ex-husband, did her in. When you're a kid, they don't tell you everything. You have to fill it in yourself." She paused again. "I didn't inherit any of May's genes, as far as I'm concerned."

"No second sight as far as you can tell," I said, "Maybe it will be in Francesca."

Denise laughed and responded, "Maybe in Francesca."

A Miscellany of Spirits–
Mysterious Beings, Ghosts, & Monsters

"The Demon in Saigon"

by Ben Nguyen

Transcription by both folklorists

Ben Nguyen told this family legend on the same day he told the Ouija board tale:

"My older sister is mentally insane now," said Ben, "The doctors diagnosed her as schizophrenic. When she was seven or eight years old, she was in her bed one day in South Vietnam. She woke up, and opened her eyes, and saw this face with horns that was looking down at her."

Jason asked, "Was she fine, up to that point?"

"She was fine," said Ben, "It was funny. She screamed. When my Mom and Dad walked in, they saw part of it. It didn't disappear when she screamed. It stayed there. My parents saw the side of the head, and then it disappeared."

Birke asked, "Is there some spirit from local folklore or mythology that might have a part in that?"

"I don't know," Ben replied, "My Mom and Dad believe it was the devil. They think it was some kind of demon. It had horns and red eyes. In Vietnamese folklore, they say to get rid of it you should leave a sharpened blade under the pillow. That'll scare it away."

This led to a discussion of folk defenses.

Birke Duncan's Epilogue

The demon's appearance had nothing to do with the family's flight from Southeast Asia. The end of the war brought about their exile. Jason asked about other measures the family took against the demon. Ben responded, "They have these little Buddhist booklets with symbolic inscriptions inside of them. Only the monks can read them. You leave them under the pillow, with the knife."

Jason Harris's Epilogue

The first time Ben told me this story, he also mentioned that his sister became interested in the occult, and that his mother partly attributed her mental illness to reading of ESP and ghost books, which practice followed soon after her demonic experience.

In addition, he told me about his "step-grandmother" who was abusive, and the only one she could "relate to" was the mentally ill sister. Ben feels that the step-grandmother's spirit may have partly influenced his sister: "Sometimes she has these weird accents [...] another voice."

Also, Ben's mother dreamed of this step-grandmother demanding back her jewelry that she'd given as a gift.

A year after Birke's transcription, Ben told me that he spoke to his mother, who insisted that neither she nor her husband actually saw the "demon." Is Ben's "false memory" then a glimpse into the unconscious human tendency to intensify a story's drama?

"Quite a Few Tales to Tell"

by Billy Utsinger

This next informant, Billy Utsinger, had so many tales to tell there wasn't enough space to include most of them. Billy was born in Youngstown, Ohio and was earning money to save up to go to the UW in computer science.

"A Remedy Against Pixies"

Billy: My grandmother was very folklorish [sic]. We came from a predominantly German background, but we had Gypsy blood in our lineage. She believed most of that stuff from her grandmother.

"For example, standing around doing housework, you keep dropping things. To her, that meant you had pixies playing with you. Small spritish [sic] spirits that followed you around, and messed with you.

"To make them go away, this is what she'd do. She'd take sea salt and put it in her left pocket. Now, supposedly to her, that made the things stop messing with you."

Jason: Did it seem to help?

Billy: I think it helped because you somewhat believed it. My grandmother believed it strongly.

Jason: Did she believe it as a kid?

Billy: Oh, yeah.

Jason: Did you ever try it yourself?

Billy: Oh, yeah, me and my sister still do it once in a while; half believing it. Not like my mother or grandmother. We like, half-believe it. It's kind of like throwing salt over your shoulder when you spill it.

Jason: So, do you believe there could be things like pixies?

Billy: I've spent enough times in the woods to see strange things out of the corner of my eye.

Billy described thinking he was seeing his dog on the right side, but then found the dog was on the other side of him.

Billy:...enough unexplained things that I would believe pretty much anything, up to a certain extent.

Billy then told about "a pagan girl, a goddess worshiper" who claimed to "see things like fairies." Then he mentioned seeing a UFO–at this point I inquired more about his parents' beliefs regarding pixies.

Jason: Did your mother or grandmother ever see a pixie?

Billy: Oh, my grandmother said she's seen them many times.

Jason: How did she describe them?

Billy: It's a corner of the eye kind of thing. If you try looking at them, they're gone. That's what she told us.

Billy then explained how his grandmother would see pixies in her garden:

Billy: It wasn't like seeing an actual thing; more like seeing a prism shape. It was in the shape of a little person–you know, with wings–but it would be like when mist goes through the air and makes rainbows.

Jason: So it wasn't really wholly substantial.

Billy: Yeah, it was there, but it was like a reflective type of light substance, but with a defined shape. She was definitely serious.

Jason: Did they seem to be nature spirits?

Billy: She said as far as she was concerned. As far as I'm concerned, they were just part of nature–a manifestation of energy that is all through wilderness areas of anything that is alive.

See Chapter Three, "Experiences with Fairies" for a discussion on connections between the environmental imagination and fairies.

After pixies, Billy told about various legend trips he'd take to sites of alleged hauntings.

Billy: Growing up, we had our share of ghost stories that we didn't really believe. We would chase [the stories] down. We had areas around our home in Pennsylvania. We had a spot where you were coming down a hill. It was a valley, and on the other side of the hill was a graveyard. Supposedly there was a witch buried there, of some sort. It was a seventeenth century graveyard, so it was pretty old. We called it the Quakers graves, because most of the people buried there were Quakers.

"As you were coming down the hill, if you put your brights on, you could see these two reflective points off something in the graveyard. And they looked like eyes, so they called them the witch's eyes. You couldn't see them every day, but you could see them once in a while. So, we would do it once in a while, just to freak people out, [and] figure out what it was.

"We looked everywhere to see what was reflecting the two headlights. So we took a car purposely that only had one headlight, to see if it only had one eye. And it didn't. It still reflected two. We used to do it all the time. We never really believed it, but it was definitely there."

Jason: Had your parents heard of that same legend?

Billy: Oh, yeah–older people did, definitely. My friend's grandmothers did, and they believed it. That was the difference. We still visually saw it, but we didn't believe it."

Billy then went on to tell about the lantern-carrying ghost of a woman who supposedly killed herself by "jumping into the locks" in the late seventeenth century because she discovered her husband had fallen in. Apparently, Billy's own mother claimed to see "someone carrying a lantern" and was "certain it was her [the ghost]."

Billy also narrated a tale about "a man named [Chester] Bedell" who supposedly "decided to renounce his religion" due to despair over "consumption or something." Allegedly, "he went outside and threw all his religious paraphernalia out the door. He said, 'If there is a

God, may snakes crawl on my grave.' And they say if you go at night there are always snakes on his grave. Now, I went there and didn't see any, but it's still a neat story nonetheless."

Billy explained the locations of various legends "It was all in Mahoning County, Trumbull County, and Beaver County. They're all connected: northeast Ohio, far west Pennsylvania. That part of the State, there's a lot of people who believe in old lore like that–a lot more than in cities. The witch's grave: there was a specific grave that was supposed to be hers. It just said, 'Wife of Jacob' because at that time they didn't necessarily put the names on graves of the women, particularly in that culture. They said it was a witch's grave because there was a cast-iron cage around the tombstone for some reason."

I asked Billy how often he tells these stories. He mainly jokes around with his sister and friends about putting sea salt in their pockets to ward off pixies.

"We definitely pass our stories along," said Billy Utsinger.

Billy then proceeded to tell of a lake monster, and alluded as well to legends of Bigfoot. Following these tales, Billy explained more about his Tinker ancestors:

"Tinkers were Welsh people instead of Romany, or whatever the Gypsies were [actually from India]. And they would travel with the Gypsies, because they were also nomadic. And they sold things like kettles and pans in little carts. And they called them tinkers, because their carts made tinkling noises. She [grandmother] said that things got messed up because the Gypsies took our family in, because they thought they had magical powers and weren't just Welsh tinkers. They realized they had them, just like the Gypsies, so they took them in and cross-bred, so it was Gypsy and Welsh together."

"So the gypsies accepted them because they had magical powers?"

"Yes, I'm sure they didn't call them magical powers," Billy replied, "but a gift– whatever."

Billy then told about the "superstition in our family about children born with the caul 'round the head; they said that they were special." Allegedly, those born with a caul in the family had second sight. His great aunt, for example, "was able to tell when women of the family were having children, whether it would be a boy or a girl. Every time someone is going to have a baby, we still talk about that."

Finally, regarding his religion, Billy explained how his "father's line was Baptist" and his "mother's line [also Protestant] is more spiritual"--the source of "all the stories." He explained that the "Gypsy stuff broadened their mind, made them think a little more, and organized religion didn't make sense anymore."

Around the Campfire–
Our Ghostly Legend-telling Session

Featuring J. Carraway Matthews, Kurt Batson, Ashley Morris, Birke Duncan, and Jason Harris

Preface by
Jason Harris

I end this series of ghostly memorates and legends with part of Birke Duncan's transcription of a legend-telling session that arose fairly spontaneously at Ashley Morris's college graduation barbecue. She told the story about seeing fairies and angels in Chapter Three.

Fireside gatherings are perhaps one of the last vestiges of communal storytelling, particularly ghost stories, in our secular society. Due to spatial limitations, I have limited transcription to a few of the ghost tales.

Transcription by
Birke Duncan
June 19, 1999

The guests talked about frightening books such as *Scary Stories to Read in the Dark,* plus TV shows like *Unsolved Mysteries* and *Sightings*, which allegedly investigated eerie phenomena. Jason stood talking to a thirty-one-year-old Englishman named J. Carraway Matthews.

Mr. Matthews said, "We lived in a small village north of London, about twenty-five miles from the outskirts I believe. It was an old village. I mean, our house alone was over four hundred years old. All the pathways that led to the church were lined by really old trees. They'd been there forever. Supposedly, they had caught some sort of disease. They stood in a brace around the church, because that's how they built it. The trees I guess had to be cut down, so they were.

"That night, we were all sleeping in bed. It was a quiet, peaceful night. All of a sudden there was the most horrible, hideous scream we had ever heard in our lives. We all got up and ran downstairs. It was my mother. She had literally felt someone, or something jump on her back, when she was walking to the restroom. Of course, it scared the heck out of her. She screamed bloody murder.

"We looked around but couldn't find anything. She felt it had jumped on her, put its arms around her neck, legs sort of wrapped around her. She physically felt it. And then it was the next day we found out they'd cut all the trees down around the ancient cemetery. A lot of people had weird things happening. That was the only physical thing."

Jason asked, "Was it because the trees had been cut down?"

"I suppose so," said Mr. Matthews. "Those trees had been put there hundreds of years ago. It was a real disruption of the earth."

Mr. Matthews also had a bad experience at a seance wherein he and his friends heard a scary, low growl.

He also said, "My godfather had a horrible seance story. He got thrown around the room. He was in a chair, got picked up, and [it] threw him right off the table."

Mr. Matthews explained to us that ghosts are a part of English experience. Owners of old manors and estates grow accustomed to the eerie presences, and regard ghosts as members of their family.

Other guests also had some contributions. Kurt Batson told this tale about the University of Washington's Suzzallo Graduate Library: "I've heard stories about these two ghosts. You know the fourth floor, with the old Dewey Decimal section and stuff like that. Supposedly, when they're closing, there's a middle aged lady just looking at the books, all the way down at the end, by the banister overlooking the third floor."

Jason Harris remarked: "That sounds like *Ghostbusters*. It [the ghost of a woman in a library depicted in the film] scared the hell out of me."

Kurt Batson continued, "She's just looking at the books, and they ask her to leave. She says, 'Okay.' She goes back down one of the aisles where there's a wall. You go back there to follow her, and she's not there."

I had also heard that legend in 1996, from a young man who worked at the library.

Kurt Batson said, "There's also supposedly a ghost down in the Children's Lit. section."

"That's a scary place," said Jason.

"Yes, it is," said Ashley Morris.

A gentleman named Bruce McCown asked, "Is that far behind, where you go behind the grating, and stuff like that?"

"Yes," said Kurt, "One of the security guards told me that when she was a student working, that she was closing one night, and kept on hearing these footsteps walking by her. There was nobody there."

Kurt related one more ghost story, about the Hansee Hall dormitory at the same university. Jason Harris and I had recorded stories told there by Leanna the pianist, and Ashley Morris.

"A long time ago," Kurt said, "Hansee was the female dorm and Clark was the male dorm. There was this janitor who fell in love with a resident on the fourth floor. The lady just did not want to go out with an old janitor. He was heart broken, so he hung himself in a stairwell going up to the fourth floor. We've heard stories of footsteps and stuff like that in the hallway at night."

Jason asked, "Who've you heard it from? Students?"

"Students," said Kurt, "I've heard it from the RA [Resident Advisor]."

This ends the transcription.

Jason and I returned to that same yard a few years later, as guests at Ashley Morris's wedding.

Analysis–Motifs, and Analogues, Structure, & The Role of Belief

The Role of Tradition

The various memorates and legends we have recorded include a variety of traditional motifs. Unless otherwise specified, they are from Stith Thompson's Motif-Index. I have not exhaustively listed every single motif. But I have indicated several to demonstrate the continuity of tradition operating in the legends and memorates we have collected.

To begin with, we'll start with ghosts–the haunting variety. Everyone knows ghosts haunt houses and castles– and we have several examples of that in our transcripts: Gordon's tale of the haunted apartments, Kerrie and Samuel's castle legends, and Dan Parr's family legend of the murdered man's ghosts are some examples. Motifs include:

E280. "Ghosts haunt buildings"

E281 "Ghosts haunt house"

E282 "Ghosts haunt castle."

In general, ghosts are conceived of as restless spirits of humans who had suffered a traumatic death, whether by accident, murder, or suicide. The restless dead constitute an international set of motifs in Stith Thompson's Motif-Index. Thus, many of the motifs of these particular ghostly accounts have numerous analogs on other traditional narratives.

We find in Dan Parr's account of the boiler room ghost that there is a historical record of a man who was murdered, and his bones deposited in the region that he haunted: "a murder had been committed in that house. There was a man that was killed; his body had been cut up and was hidden in the hot water tank which was right outside the bathroom where the footsteps had stopped" ("Murdered person cannot rest in grave." E413.).

The ghost of Hansee Hall reported at the barbecue also involves a suicide of a lovesick janitor; and a woman committed suicide next to one of the haunted units in the Larch apartment house Gordon managed. Gordon also asserts he had heard that economic desperation had driven men to kill themselves in the Meany Hotel: "There were quite a bit of suicides there in the thirties and during the Depression" (411.1.1. "Suicide cannot rest in grave."). That the spirits of the dead would urge Gordon and his co-workers to "jump" is consistent with traditions in the United States (E.266.2. "Ghost leads people to commit suicide." Baughman). Marta, though she could not vouch for the veracity, told me that "our next door neighbor says the previous owner's son had killed himself in the house." All of these examples indicate that the traditions of people dying traumatically and then becoming ghosts, were clearly in circulation at the end of the twentieth century.

The conjunction between knowledge of human violence and the phenomena of ghosts implies an associative, or even a causal connection. Because we do not have the means to establish whether ghosts actually exist apart from the imagination of informants, our analysis must limit itself to interaction between the mind and its environment–both real and imagined. In much the same way that dreams formulate and display the dreamer's hopes and anxieties, it is possible that ghosts derive from the hallucinatory faculty of the brain, which may sometimes function to express and expel tensions similar to that of the dreamer.

But we do not need to plumb the depths of psychology to interpret ghost memorates and legends; for the stories themselves perform the same essential functions that the ghosts do. That is to say, if the function of the ghost of Chris's grandfather is to reassure Chris that there is an afterlife, then the story of the experience–whether real or imaginary–serves the same function.

Similarly, for Gordon to be haunted by ghosts of suicidal hotel guests from the Depression era serves to remind Gordon of the intensity of human suffering during that period. The haunting features a history lesson. Or rather, the memorate itself when combined with the contextual information produces the form of a legend, which in popular circulation functions as an unofficial history. We do not really need ghosts, as long as we have ghost stories.

The persistence of traditions–such as that the person who dies traumatically will return as a ghost–suggest that there is a mindset, a set of conventions, or social conditions which has persisted historically. In other words, people are still as disturbed by murder and suicide as they used to be in ancient times. An event of murder or suicide haunts the survivors. Such an occasion is not soon forgotten.

Similarly, we find the continued urgency of economic factors. From the Depression-era suicides narrated by Gordon Dwyer to Ben Nguyen's account of his Vietnamese grandfather revealing the location of hidden money–wealth clearly figures as an integral feature of life. Indeed, in a sense, money is the barrier between life and death. To be economically deprived is in many cultures to be virtually dead–to have no autonomy or security. Thus, when Ben Nguyen's mother dreams of her father's ghost, the dream expresses the dire necessity of finding the money, and emphasizes that the wealth is an intrinsic family link. What is the bridge between one generation and the next after death? The answer, it seems, is inheritance.

As is common with legends and memorates, many of these occur on an interface between the wild and civilized realms.[5] That is also known as the perilous periphery or the edge. Samuel Barton's memorate experience of the power of fairies near a plowed field is a perfect example of this dynamic. Mr. Barton emphasizes the very confrontation between natural and cultivated when he describes how those "charming little trees [...] in fields [...] had been completely plowed around them."

Neither I nor Mr. Barton could identify the exact species of trees which would be fascinating to ascertain–according to Katharine Briggs the trees which are most often the haunts of fairies are the Hawthorn and May trees. However, "solitary trees and bushes" of other varieties may be fairy residences as well."[6] Regardless, the powers of the otherworld, the world that is not cultivated by humanity, assert themselves near the trees in a seemingly harmless, yet potent manner. By pushing back the car, the fairies declare the boundary between their sacred trees and modern technology.

In contrast to the peaceful observation of fairy property in Mr. Barton's memorate of a legendary encounter with fairy power, J. Carraway Matthews's memorate of his mother's attack by a spirit is the other side of the coin. Notably, Mr. Matthews evaluates the action of cutting down the trees near the church as "a real disruption of the earth." Thus, the taboo has been broken. The civilized world has attacked the boundary of nature–the ancient trees perish, and their guardians or inhabitants strike out against the aggressors who have upset the balance between the wild and the cultivated.

The show of force in Mr. Barton's and Mr. Matthews's accounts are appropriate to the themes. While the manipulation of the car is an interesting and harmless display of power, the invisible assault on Mr. Matthews's mother is not. The former supernatural incident is a sign of symbiosis; humans may experience wondrous, positive things if they respect the fairies. The latter supernatural situation, described by Mr. Matthews, signifies hostility and transgression; just as the humans have crossed the line against the trees and their invisible inhabitants, so the balance is upset, and the spirits assault the living.

Located on a similar interface between the wild and civilized, the "knocker" warns Birke and Andrew that the underground is not humanity's proper domain. There is a whole tradition of spirits known as "knockers" which may be either malicious or helpful to miners, while others suggest that they are the aboriginal spirits of some strange troglodyte race.[7] A mine is clearly an interface between the wild and civilized domains since like a canal or furrow, it is a pathway devised by people to explore, tame and exploit the natural world.

In addition, the mining ghost emphasizes the danger of mining conditions–it functions as a signifier for the sometimes deadly conditions in mines where many men, women, and children have lost their lives. Knockers are known to appear to warn miners of imminent danger (Baughman F 456.1.2.2.4). An accident may have occurred in the mind, and the ghost haunts it for that reason (E275.1 "Ghost haunts mine after tragedy.") One may also view the ghost as the hallucinatory projection of the attitudes of Birke Duncan and Andrew Brinkman.[8] Birke was in the frame of mind to expect trouble; he suggests Andrew will get them lost. Andrew has already invoked the presence of evil, "that goat was evil! It wanted to kill me," and he is the first one to see the spirit.

Incidentally, Birke did not see any unexplained images or ghosts when he returned to the same Norwegian mine two years later.

What is conspicuously missing in these tales is the malice that is traditionally common among revenants. No one is punished, at least not severely. Take for example Ben Nguyen's account of the old man who appears in the dream of his friend's mother.[9] The appearance is a mere warning, yet topically it is associated with the motif "Return from the dead to punish the disturber of grave" (E235.6).

Even the ghost or spirit that jumps on the back of Mr. Matthews's mother causes no lasting harm–though this is one motif filed under the section of malevolent revenants (E260 "Other malevolent revenants." E262 "Ghost rides on man's back.").

The only malignancy among ghosts that dangerously rears its head are the spirits that harass Ben Nguyen and his friends after their Ouija board experiences. The use of Buddhist chant tapes is a remedy in the example of magical protection against revenants. The tapes themselves are a technological update of the prayer book, and thus their efficacy seems to be associated with the following motif: "Ghost cannot pass cross or prayer book" E434.8. Interestingly, Buddhism rather than any Western religion, figured prominently in exorcising the spirits that were allegedly encountered. The hauntings in Gordon's apartment house, at least as far as the upstairs apartment, ended due to a Buddhist exorcism ("Ghost exorcized [sic] and laid" E443).

By far, the most threatening encounter is Ben Nguyen's family legend of the demonic being which threatened his sister. Notably, Ben's stories are generally full of danger–which may derive from the conflicted nature of the Vietnamese environment. Birke Duncan suggests the influence of war. Dr. Sallet in *"Les Esprits Malfaisants"* (Evil-doing spirits) points out how evil spirits are prominent in Binh-Thuan, an area characterized by ethnic tensions, epidemics, and a chaotic landscape.[10] Dr. Sallet presents a popular Vietnamese phrase which suggests the savagery of these spirits: *"Les tigres sont nombreux [...] ce sont les fantomes"* (The tigers are numerous [...] they're the ghosts.). In a conversation, Ben told me that about ninety percent of Vietnamese people living in Vietnam believe in things like this demon–replete with horns and evil intentions.

Several international motifs apply to Ben's demonic memorate. Specifically, the use of metal and knife against the fairies is pertinent, though this demon would not usually be called a fairy (Baughman F384.2 "Steel powerful against fairies." F384.2 "Knife powerful against fairies.") Especially significant is that the exact charm employed against the demon is used to prevent fairy abduction of a child: F321.2 (b) "A knife under the pillow will protect child from exchange by fairies."

Also, the red eyes of the demon are apparently described in some fairy descriptions (F239.[11] "Fairy has red eyes."). Birke's research has yielded the following motifs, which are related to the folk defenses against spirits in Ben's tales as well:

G 272.3"Knife in bed as protection against witches."

E 434.7"Knives as protection from revenants."

E 434.8"Ghosts cannot pass across prayer book."

E 439.1"Revenant forced away by shooting."

Publications of Vietnamese folklore provide related precedents for Ben's memorates. Regarding the consequent mental illness of Ben's sister, the Hmong (who inhabit Laos, Thailand, and Vietnam) have a tradition that "several types of spirits commonly affect the mental health of individual"[11] Similarly, the Moi, a mountain tribe who dwell in the forests of the Moi plateau in Vietnam, believe that the delirium that results from marsh fever is "the incarnation of an evil spirit."[12] The Hmong treat a child with particular caution because it is believed malign entities may steal "its spirit."[13] While according to basic Hmong traditions evil spirits "live in areas not populated by people," others believe spirits can be any- where and there are accounts of these malign entities crossing the border between the wild and the civilized.[14]

In fact there is a Vietnamese tale, "The Cat Which Became a Queen," which tells of an evil spirit that enters an open window in the form of a black cat. Boldly entering the domestic sphere–like Ben's demon– the cat slays a queen, and then takes on her form. The doppelganger then acts as a succubus, draining the vital powers of the king.[15] Notably, Ben mentions the monks' warning that an open window is vulnerable to spiritual intrusion.

In *"The Rope Ghost and "Histoire du demon de Xuong Giang"*[The Story of the Demon of Xuong Giang]--both Vietnamese folktales telling of demonic spirits–there are references to a "king of hell," which may be the equivalent of Satan in Vietnamese folklore.[16] However, this "king of hell" appears to be more concerned with directing other malicious spirits and deciding on matters of guilt and punishment rather than personally harassing an individual. The latter tale also indicates that the ghost of a murdered person may return as a demon, whose powers are greater than ordinary revenants, and which can take many forms. It is unclear, however, whether Ben's parents are asserting that the spirit was one of many devils or demons, or a primary one: "My Mom and Dad believe it was the devil. They think it was some kind of demon."

Vietnamese folklore also bears upon Ben's comments (after the account of his grandfather's spirit appearing in a dream) that his friends from "Asian families" often have ghostly encounters but for "my other friends of other races it doesn't [...]". In *Beyond the East Wind–Legends & Folktales of Vietnam* Jewell Coburn asserts that: "To many Vietnamese, the community consists of the living, the very personal spirits of dead relatives and intimate friends, and the less personal spirits of nature–all having the potential of contact with each other" (94). An example of interaction between the world of the living and the dead figures in *Under the Starfruit Tree– Folktales from Vietnam*. The dead spirit of Phat Sinh's lover, Le Nuong, appears to him in a dream ("The Story of Le Nuong"). Another tale, "Truong Ba and the Butcher's Skin", in the same book relates how "people believed that an individual might carry the spirit of a deceased person" just as Ben hypothesizes the abusive step-grandmother has possessed his sister (99-101). [17]

Stith Thompson catalogs an entire set of motifs for "The Friendly Return from the Dead," as well as the more vengeful varieties. Thus our many accounts of ghosts of dead relatives are in good company: E320 "Dead relatives friendly return." The ghost of Chris Aynesworth's grandfather and Mrs. Duncan's father represent the motif of the friendly ghostly return. The return of Ben Nguyen's grandfather in his mother's dream to communicate where he sequestered away the money is a recurrent motif: E371 "Return from the dead to reveal hidden treasure." Then there are seemingly neutral ghosts like the lantern-carrying ghost seen by Billy's mother, which is itself an international motif (599.7 "Ghost carries lantern.")

Among our ghostly forms we find the soul, astral body, or spirit appearing in memorates of out-of-body experiences. Steve's report of the experience of his ex-girlfriend is a classic example of the belief of how the soul may leave the body during sleep (E721.1 "Soul wanders from body in sleep"). What is unusual about this account, however, is that there was a witness–the girlfriend acts as an outside observer. This introduces a degree of objectivity, which contrasts with most out-of-body memorates. Steve's account is legendary, or rather the cancer survivor's abilities are legendary, since rumor of his talents has traveled to several people and persisted over time.

When this spiritual double appears it is usually a sign of imminent or coincident death, and is referred to as a person's wraith or fetch.[18] We may distinguish wraiths generally from ghosts by using the Scottish differentiation that Andrew Lang cites in *The Book in Dreams and Ghosts*: "'Spirits of the living' is the Highland term for the appearances of people who are alive and well–but [living] elsewhere. The common Highland belief is that they show themselves to second-sighted persons [...]" (84). Lang's expression of "alive and well" is hasty however, since many accounts of wraiths are contemporaneous with death-bed scenes. We have various examples from our informants of this tradition of the spirits of the living, as well as testimonies of second sight (D 1825.1 "Second sight). Leanna's tale of her grandmother seeing her adopted son is a classic example of a wraith. Leanna emphasizes that the time when the grandmother claimed to see the apparition, and the death of Jimmy, was identical.

Wraiths are known to appear in dreams as well as to the vigilant eyes of the conscious, yet there does not seem to be an exact motif number for this recurring theme–the general appearances of ghosts (whether a revenant or a wraith) in dreams. Regardless, Mrs. Duncan's dream of her friend, Mrs. Copeland, dressed in a particular outfit the night she died is a perfect example of this tradition. In addition, to view the other person's wraith is generally considered to be a death omen for the person whom the apparition resembles (E 723.6 "Appearance of his wraith as announcement of person's death.")[19]

All wraiths are not cut from the same cloth. For instance in "The Waff"--a tale collected by Katharine Briggs –we find that a man avoids his imminent death by scolding his wraith when it appears, and "the waff slunk off abashed and the evil design with which it came there was brought happily to nought."[20]

"Waff" is the Yorkshire term for wraith. This wraith appears to have a personality and an agenda of its own rather than merely being an emanation of the man, as is often the case with wraiths. Wraiths described as appearing near the time of a person's death usually seem to be identified closely with the individual's own psyche or soul.

The German term for this double is *Dopfelganger* or Doppelganger (double-goer or double-walker). The loan word in English is doppelganger. Lily Weise-Aall maintains that doppelganger lore is a "very variable phenomenon in folklore and probably not ultimately based on any single unified belief."[21] In the nineteenth century, several famous writers are reputed to have seen their doubles: Johann Wolfgang von Goethe, Heinrich Hoffmann, Guy de Maupassant, and Percy Bysshe Shelley.[22] The Catholic Church recognizes the double as a kind of spiritual projection known as "bilocation."[23] From the Scottish Highlands to Finland and Norway, there are accounts of "doubles and shadow figures" sometimes thought to be spiritual guardians.[24] This "waff" in the tale collected by Katharine Briggs, however, appears as a malign entity.

Marta's account of the doppelganger is similar to the "waff"; it appears to be an autonomous entity, which adopts the appearance of another for its own ends, inscrutable as they may be. The doppelganger is generally conflated with the wraith in popular legends, as well as encyclopedias of folklore and motif indexes. Yet there are particular strands of tradition that distinguish the doppelganger from the idea of a spiritual double centered around a particular individual. Katharine Briggs cites seventeenth century scholar Robert Kirk's work *The Secret Commonwealth* in which Kirk includes these doubles or co-walkers among the fairies in Scottish lore. Allegedly gleaning his observations from the perceptions of people with second sight, Kirk claims: "They call this

Reflex-man a Co-walker, every way like the Man [...] haunting him as his shadow [...] both before and after the Originall [sic] is dead [...]."[25] Kirk's "Co-walker" seems to be a fixed form that mirrors the human, so it is not identical to the being described in Marta's memorate.

Though Ernest W. Baughman equates the wraith with the doppelganger in his *Type and Motif-Index of the Folktales of England and North America*, there is a tradition of a doppelganger that is not the "astral body" or spiritually bound to a particular person; instead it may assume the identity of an individual and then kill the original. Unfortunately there is difficulty in finding sources and scholarship on this particular strand of the doppelganger tradition. The entry in the *Larousse Dictionary of World Folklore* does mention, however, that the doppelganger "can assume volition and a form of its own" (148). Informed readers are encouraged to share their knowledge–write a letter or email–regarding the doppelganger on this point.[26]

One Mongolian tale, not unlike the legend of Asmodeus's adoption of Solomon's shape or the shape-shifting evil Vietnamese spirit in "The Cat That Became a Queen", relates how a devil figure (Shimnu) assumes the form of a man's son. The doppelganger arrives simultaneously at the household when the son returns home from the wars–tries to insinuate itself into the family (it knows the son's past even better than the son himself); a ploy which ultimately fails.[27]

The tradition of the insidious doppelganger may partly derive from Greek mythology and Talmudic lore. In the myth of Amphitryon, Zeus desires the warrior's wife, Alomene. The god impersonates the hero in his absence at war–the result is that the hero Heracles is born the son of Zeus; also born is the twin brother Iphicles–thought to be Amphitryon's son rather than divine progeny (D658.2 "Transformation to husband's (lover's) form to seduce woman). [28]

A related legend in the Talmud concerns Solomon and Asmodeus (Ashmedai). Acting under the command of

God to punish King Solomon, Asmodeus the lord of demons usurps Solomon's throne and disguises himself in Solomon's form, in order to deceive others and seduce Solomon's wives, and "mother Bathsheba."[29]

Baughman notes that the appearance of the wraith, which he equates with the doppelganger, in "many instances have no significance of death to come" (197). Thus the sight of the doppelganger or wraith of John by Marta's brother seems to be one of those neutral circumstances. In fact, there is no clear purpose or function of Marta's memorates, other than perhaps a kind of projected anxiety of being caught out in the shed with her boyfriend. Perhaps there is fear of seduction by her brother's friends that partly motivates Marta's vision in her bedroom. A closer examination of family dynamics might have led to other possible conclusions as well. Notably, Marta claims never to have heard of the tradition of wraiths or doppelgangers.

Besides Marta's doppelganger, the phenomena she describes are reminiscent of poltergeist experiences. The hurling of objects (the reindeer) and general mischief inside the house with the television, the lock, and the knockings and rappings have all been recorded in Baughman's Type and Motif Index:

F473.1 "Poltergeist throws objects"

F 473.5.5 (a)"Knockings and rappings that cannot be traced"

F 473.5 (b)"Footsteps"

Chris Aynesworth's experience with his doors are also associated with poltergeists. Mr. Barton's tale of the ghost in Dunsany castle moving furniture around is a poltergeist-like ghostly action (E599.7.6 "Ghosts move furniture")

The fact that the poltergeist raises havoc with the television (the spirits in the 1982 movie *Poltergeist* behave similarly) in Marta's memorat emphasizes the ability of folklore to keep up with modern technology. Just as gremlins found their way onto airplanes, so poltergeists have discovered the television set. I once heard a memorate about a pixie that caused trouble with a microwave. Despite earlier predictions of how the industrial revolution would banish the fairies and goblins, clearly there is enough anxiety, chaos, and imagination in modern technology to provide fertile ground for the traditional spirits of folklore.

The ability to see the future and spirits like doppelgangers, revenants, and wraiths is one of the features of second sight.[30] Informants whose tales overtly included second sight are Billy Utsinger, Denise (Francesca's mother), and Mrs. Duncan. As Anne Ross explains in *The Folklore of the Scottish Highlands*, second sight is a dubious gift: "it comes from them at random and usually against their will" (38). Notably, "the power of seeing a person's *Dopfelganger* or 'other self'" is an aspect of second sight.

There is a similar belief in Norway: in a survey of one hundred and ten respondents in 1960, most people stated that only individuals with second sight have a double, although some respondents claimed everyone has one.[31] The burden of such a gift is to carry the knowledge of approaching death of oneself or others. Related to the precognition of second sight is the tradition that visions of the future, and communications with the spirit world often come in dreams.[32] Examples of this belief dramatically figure in Ben Nguyen's story of his friend Robin, to whose mother an old man's ghost appears in a dream, as well as of Mrs. Duncan's sight of her deceased friend, and the dream of Ben's own mother–revealing hidden money.

There are some motifs in other informants' accounts of ghosts that seem not to have been catalogued, yet they have related precedents. For instance, in Scotland evil spirits are known to be black and are referred to as "Bukka-dhu." And we find the Ouija board "demon" that Chris Aynesworth encounters has a black shape.[33]

Another example of a recurring, undocumented motif is the observation in memorats and legends that ghosts move by unusual locomotion, not walking. Rachel, the young woman from Australia, describes the ghost she sees as moving in the air: "she was back a little ways [...] just four feet off the ground."[34] Gordon Dwyer's account

391

of the moving shadow with the hood is a similar example of peculiar locomotion.[35]

Structural Analysis

Among the legends, we find there are features of traditional structure in the narratives as well as motifs. Memorates are "legends-in-waiting," so to speak. They potentially may become legends at any time once they are more frequent and communal rather than isolated and personal. Such was the case with the ghost in Suzzallo library at the University of Washington. It also applies to "The Troll Tale" by Garrett Vance and Holly Luidl Wyatt.

For the purposes of this study, we will align memorates with legends in terms of structure. Referring to W.F.H. Nicolaisen's structural studies of legend, Timothy Tangherlini outlines the structural features in *Interpreting Legend*: "the legend may encompass as many as six distinct structural elements, these being abstract, orientation, complicating action, evaluation, result, and coda, or as few as two, namely orientation and complicating action" (10). Many of the memorates and legends we have compiled may strike the reader as amorphous, but if one focuses on the complicating situation and then looks for orientation and result, one will soon see the basic structure of a legend is present. Indeed, one can find at least one example of each category of legend structure within the different accounts we have selected. An example of the abstract occurs within Billy Utsinger's statement: "There's always been a superstition in our family about children born with a caul 'round the head; they said that they were special." In other words, the abstract is a synopsis of the legend, which the storyteller elaborates upon contextually through the orientation, complicating action, evaluation, result, and coda.

A clear example of the "complicating action" occurs in a memorate like that of Samuel Barton: "this young lady [...] drove the car to the bottom of this slope. Then she took her feet off the gas and her hands off the driving wheel and the car rose back up [pause] to the top of this grade [pause for drama again] all by itself." Here we clearly see the shift between the orientation–the context of normalcy–and the complicating situation–the introduction of the supernatural. In fact, one may identify a key word which, obvious as it may seem, announces the complicating action and is consistent enough to be worthy of notice: "then."

One may find examples of the association between the word "then" and the complicating situation in a legend or memorate throughout the performances of our informants. Birke's performance of his haunted mine story likewise emphasizes the importance of the word, "then." "[Andrew Brinkman] looked to the left and said, 'Hi, how are you?' Then he yelled, 'Eee-yaah! There's a human head in there!'"

In Chris Aynesworth's recital of the memorate concerning his grandfather's ghost, it is precisely in the sentence containing "then," that the preternatural is introduced: "I tried to sleep, but I couldn't. And then, there was no sound, but my eyes were closed." Interestingly, the sentence containing "then" is rather inexact; it is not clear what is taking place, but it is clear that something bizarre is occurring, which is elaborated in the narrator's next sentence: "It was like someone flashed a camera in front of my eyes."

It is as though the word "then" is sufficient to relate the introduction of the fantastic. "Then" is the semantic dividing line that invokes the metaphysical transgression of the border between normalcy and the preternatural, which is the hallmark of the memorate or legend. Indubitably, "then" serves as a potent indicator of the complicating situation in a legend narrative.

Rhetorically and structurally, the informant's performance of a legend helps to define its borders. Take for example Denise's account of her grandmother's second sight– in particular the meeting with the psychic whom the family had hired to help find the grandmother's (May's) missing older sister. When Birke and I prod her for details, she just isn't interested. For Denise, the importance of the family legend was the revelation of her grandmother's second sight, not the gruesome tale of murder, and the momentum of her performance comes to a halt at the coda: "That, to me, is kind of intriguing."

Structurally, there is an anomaly in Samuel Barton's account of Dunsany castle. Everyone is familiar with the tripartite structure of fairy tales, the law of three–how the third attempt, or challenge, or brother, or princess will result in success or at least involve some sort of progress. This tradition of the importance of three has influenced the basic structure of much literature and music, not to mention theories of philosophy and history. Thesis, antithesis, and synthesis; strophe, antistrophe, and epode–the basic threefold structure is well known in formal rhetoric and aesthetics as well as popular narratives and superstitions. Axel Olrik identifies the threefold aspect of oral narrative as his "epic laws."[36] How many times does Chris Aynesworth find his door open? Three times. On what night does Steve experience the breathing ghost? The third night. How many times does Samuel Barton find his door open? Four times. Thus Barton's memorate is unusual in violating the conventional rule of three. The numeral three figures prominently in examples beyond the ones I mentioned. If you skim the transcripts, you will find the number three occurring with surprising frequency.

The Role of Belief

The dynamic between Billy Utsinger and me represents one of the many assumptions about legend-telling sessions, and in this case at least proves true. As Henning Sehmsdorf reports in *Scandinavian Folk Belief & Legend*: "According to Linda Degh, the recital of the legend usually takes the form of a conversation" (18). Sehmsdorf also includes another reference which is pertinent here, with regard to the role of belief, he quotes from the article "Legends and Belief" by Linda Degh & Andrew Vazsonyi: "As much as it seems proven that the personal belief of the participants in the legend process is irrelevant, it also seems to be a rule that general reference to belief is an inherent and most outstanding feature of the folk legend" (18). Among all the informants, Billy presents us with the most interesting and articulate statements concerning the role of belief. He is referring in particular to a witch legend when he makes this assertion, but it might be applied to his other legends as well:

Jason: Had your parents heard of that same legend?

Billy: Oh, yeah–older people did, definitely. My friend's grandmothers did, and they believed it. That was the difference, we still visually saw it, but we didn't believe it.

This is a fascinating statement for several reasons. Billy describes an ethnological shift in the folk beliefs of his community that the 1999 Gallup poll did not reveal by statistics alone. Billy's attitude shows that wholehearted, conscious belief is far from necessary for a tradition bearer. For Billy and his peers, it seems that entertainment and an interest in family and local history are the major factors, which stimulate the accumulation and the exercise of his repertoire. In addition, Billy negates the commonplace notion that "seeing is believing." Billy and his peers are scrutinizing the perceptual outlines of a legend with more than their eyes. There is a generation gap between the two attitudes of the "older people" and the younger people who include Billy among their number.

Belief, or the consciousness of belief, seems to have steadily gone underground in the twentieth century. Notably, Billy Utsinger explained to me that his sister related the pixy belief to their friends when they were drunk–a form of repression appears to censor the transmission of this folk belief in sober situations (F.384.1 "Salt powerful against fairies.").

Dr. Hazard Adams of the University of Washington's Comparative Literature Department encountered an attitude similar to Billy's amalgam of belief and skepticism, when he was in Ireland about 1951.[37] He had the following exchange with his housekeeper, Nellie Murphy:

"Tell me, Nellie, do you believe in the fairies?"

"No, I don't believe in them...but they're there."

Nellie's statement suggests that her belief is ultimately irrelevant to the objective reality of the fairies, or rather the tradition's power is so deeply ingrained culturally and psychologically that conscious belief or disbelief is not the deciding factor.

Similarly, Billy is not about to stop telling the many legends and folk beliefs he learned. He may not believe them, but they are part of his heritage: "We definitely pass our stories along."

The very paradoxical nature of Billy Utsinger and Nellie Murphy's statements also indicates the complexity of belief. Note, for example, that while Billy states "we never really believed it" regarding the witch's ghost, he asserts he and his sister "like half-believe" the salt remedy. Thus, even from an informant's own mouth, he cannot conclusively draw a rigid stance of belief or disbelief, as Billy says, "I would pretty much believe anything up to a certain extent."

Note the large variety of religious beliefs among our informants–they include Catholics, Protestants, Buddhists, atheists, agnostics, and spiritualists. Clearly the presence of traditional lore transcends any particular doctrine that accompanies one's upbringing. However, among our informants we do encounter a variety of different attitudes, yet as Degh, Sehmsdorf, and Vazsonyi seem to agree this is a feature of legend-bearers that is observed throughout a range of different cultures.

However, this is not to say that reserved skepticism or enthusiastic belief produces identical results in terms of performance. At least in the case of memorates. Take Steve's ghost memorate, for example. Steve's tale of his initial bold disbelief is very much like the tale-type "The Youth Who Wanted to Learn What Fear Is" (AT 326): "I thought it was great, I was going to stay in the blue room with the ghosts and check it out, because I'm a non-believer."[38] After learning what "heart-pounding" fear is, in Steve's case, the intensity of his belief, or lack thereof, appears to directly correspond to the frequency of recitation of the tale. As the experience with the breathing ghost became less immediate, Steve's performance of that memorate decreased:

401

Steven: The next day I was saying, 'I'm a believer' and told that stories a hundred times in a week because it was so fresh. This was actually ten or eleven years ago, and I hadn't really thought about it till talking to you.

Jason: So, it wore off after a while?

Steven: Yeah, you know, after not seeing a ghost every night. With time you have to question things, but at the time you couldn't convince me other than there was something there.

Despite the decade and the decline of belief intervening between Steve's experience and his performance of his tale to me, his storytelling was animated and dramatic. Steven emphasized several times that he remembered how his "heart was pounding."

Clearly, there is a poetics of superstition at work, which produces the feeling of emotional immediacy despite temporal and sensory distance. Like the Romantic notion of "emotion recollected in tranquility" conveyed by William Wordsworth, there is a similar, if not identical, impulse at work with raconteurs of memorates and legends. I would argue that Wordsworth's most intense poetic moments in *The Prelude* in fact are stimulated by a sense of the uncanny. It is the primal feeling of superstition that is the root of many a creative work. Superstitious dread is assuredly an aspect of the sublime.

Conclusion

Besides individual psychology and upbringing, the media contributes to the frame of reference that influences our informants' beliefs. Notably, Marta, when describing the poltergeist activity out in the shed, refers to the 1982 movie, *Poltergeist.* Similarly, Ben Nguyen invokes the 1973 movie *The Exorcist*–where a Ouija board leads to demonic possession, in the preamble to his own memorates of chaos surrounding Ouija board experiences. The media has popularized the Ouija board, from books on the subject, to the 1986, 1989, and 1995 *Witchboard* movies, which exaggerate the antisocial and fantastic lore of the Ouija board.

Birke notes that the guests at Ashley Morris's barbecue incorporated print and television media into their vision of ghostly matters: "The guests talked about frightening books like *Scary Stories to Read in the Dark*, plus TV shows like *Unsolved Mysteries* and *Sightings*, which allegedly investigated eerie phenomena." That transcript also shows that I brought up the 1984 movie *Ghostbusters* in response to the Suzzallo library legend.

Significantly, when Steve Clemens explains what constitutes his attitude toward the supernatural, he places movies and television on an equal footing with his more direct experiences with people: "...it was just experiences: what you see on televisions, movies, and talking to people. I believe I have an open mind about it and definitely take the stance: 'I'll believe it when I see it.'" Thus, rather than viewing TV and movies as a fantasy world set apart from empirical reality, our informants invoke media references to articulate their own personal stories. Apparently, older, traditional folklore and contemporary, technological popular culture have merged into a legendary matrix from which modern storytellers shape their tales.

The final consideration with regard to belief is how it affects the dynamic between collector and informant. Rather than assuming a debunking pose, wholehearted belief, or–God forbid–gullibility, it seems that healthy skepticism combined with an open mind is a favorable position for the collector to adopt when interviewing informants. After all, this is not The *X-Files*; folklorists are concerned with the stories, their content, and performance, not with objective reality or falsity of claims of folk belief. Furthermore, informants like to challenge the borders of a collector's worldview; not how Ben and Steve both make such challenges. "Do you believe in ghosts?" Steve asks me. Similarly, Ben asserts: "I'll prove you wrong right here" when I suggest the Ouija board primarily involves the unconscious mind. Just as legends and memorates express anxieties and energies on the edge of the secure and the mundane, so the bearers of these traditional narratives sometimes like to test the boundaries of their listener's rational complacency.

The persistence and wide dispersions of traditional conceptions of ghosts and spiritual beings in the Northwest attest to the ongoing concern with death as a compelling topic. In particular, there are indications that the large volume of traditional material regarding ghosts may be a symptom of cultural repression. That is to say, we see ghosts because as individuals and a society we do not articulately communicate about death. In a 1999 *Time* magazine issue an article asserts that death is "The Last Taboo."

Half of Americans say they want their family and friends to carry out their Final wishes, yet 75% of them have never taken the time to articulate what those desires might be, according to a new study by the National Hospice Foundation. Surprisingly parents find it easier to talk to their children about such issues as sex than to talk with their own parents about dying with dignity.

By and large, death and dying are worrisome topics– connected to them are threats to one's physical and financial wellbeing. Will one die naturally, or suffer an accident, or be murdered? Will we leave a secure inheritance behind to our children? Is grandfather okay? Does he still love me? Is there an afterlife? Concerns like these are central to the emotive content of the legends and memorates we have recorded. As our campfire legend-telling session indicates, people are definitely still commonly and communally telling tales of ghostly folklore. Our raconteurs offer you speculation, and concrete evidence that traditional tales of the spirit world are with us today.

Ghosts will haunt us long into the new millennium.

Glossary

Abstract: Introduction of an oral story via an undetailed summary.

Angel: Holy Messenger of God. Not to be confused with fairies.

Anecdote: A personal history, usually told orally, often humorous.

Animism: Religious belief that everything in creation has a spirit.

Anti-Memorat: A firsthand account of a mistaken perception of a supernatural presence.

Anti-Tale: A third person fictional narrative with the elements of a ghost story, but a sudden plot twist at the end turns it into a joke.

Banshee: An Irish female spirit who appears shrieking and moaning, as a harbinger of someone's death.

Bukka-dhu: Scottish word for "black spirits." Presented shockingly in the 1990 movie, *Ghost*.

Changeling: A fairy or witch's ugly offspring substituted for a mother's real baby.

Cherub, collectively Cherubim: Warrior angels of the Old Testament with a human face, bull or lion's body, and eagle's wings. Later depicted artistically as winged babies.

Coda: Final tag that concludes an oral tale.

Complication of Action: An element comes up that will progress directly to conflict and climax in a story.

Context: Circumstances of a storytelling experience, pertaining to time, place, lighting, mood, and date.

Cultural-Centered Belief Theory: People believe what their culture informs them about the nature of belief and reality.

Doppelganger: A loan word from German for double walker, or double goer. A person's double, or way of appearing in two places at once. Also known as a Co-walker or Reflex-man in Highland Scottish lore.

Dryad: Tree spirit taking on human form.

Edge: The unsafe zone on the border of the safe area, where strange adventures can happen.

Experience-Centered Belief Theory: People believe their experiences, which then verify cultural information about a specific belief.

Fairy: Other worldly nature or household spirit, similar to animism beliefs.

Fairy Land: Parallel universe.

Festive: Like a feast or festival: a time-out-of-time for merriment and traditions linked to the occasion, but not appropriate at other times.

Fetch: A spirit of the living, or astral projection of a person. Also known as bilocation.

Ghost: Spirit of a dead person.

Gift: A magical power, or psychic talent.

Good People, The: A term for fairies.

Hulder (plural Huldre): Norwegian term for the hidden or invisible people, who occasionally become visible.

Jump Tale: A fictitious scary story with a conclusion that startles listeners.

Kappa or river child: Japanese folklore creature, frog-like humanoids with turtle shells.

Knocker or Tommyknocker: The ghost of a miner.

Legend: A story told as true, usually in the third person in order to convey a lesson or warning.

Legend Trip: An informal journey to explore the site of a local legend. It combines physical activity with oral tradition.

Leprechaun: An Irish fairy cobbler and trickster, guardian of a pot of gold at the end of the rainbow.

Memorat (or Memorate): A personal experience story about the supernatural.

Motif: An element or theme that remains the same in different tales.

Naturalist Folk Belief Theory: Natural features appear "super" natural and alive to human perception.

Objective Correlative: A specific place or object that evokes emotion with its symbolism. Examples can include a haunted house, for fear of the supernatural; or an empty, furnished bedroom, to imply a tragedy.

Orientation: The part of a story that provides the background that leads up to the main action.

Other, The: A social outsider, or a mysterious being.

Out of Body Experience: A report of viewing oneself or surroundings away from one's own bodily point of view.

Perilous Periphery: Another term for the danger zone, or no man's land, where the experiencer finds the supernatural or the threat. An area of interface between civilization and chaos.

Poltergeist (German for noisy spirit): An entity or astral projection of a person that causes accidents or mischief.

Pwca (or pooka): Welsh version of the English trickster Puck. A fairy and a mischievous will o'the wisp.

Raconteur: A storyteller, especially one with great skill as a theatrical entertainer.

Resolution: The climax of a story and its aftermath.

Revenant: A ghost, especially of a specific person, as opposed to an impersonal spook with no known identity.

Second Sight: The psychic talent of being able to see the supernatural. Also known as "The Third Eye."

Simultaneous Informatory Experience: When two separate events coincide, and form a link to the supernatural. For instance, a clock stops at the moment its donor dies. Dramatic examples include remote visitation of a dying person to friends or relatives at the moment of their death.

Theosophy: A dramatic, ecstatic spiritual movement of the nineteenth century.

Tradition: A skill, ritual, narrative, or practice transmitted from the experienced generation to the younger generation.

Troll: Scandinavian nature monster, quasi-personification of rocks, mountains, and trees.

Trooping Fairies: A group of male fairies in some expedition of mischief or ritual.

Wraith or Waff: Someone's double that appears at the moment of their demise. This is a common motif in Simultaneous Informatory Experiences.

Bibliography

Prologue
The Story of the *Standard*

Perry, Fredi. Port Madison, Washington Territory 1884-1889. Bremerton, Washington. Perry Publishing, 1989.

Thompson, Stith. Motif-Index of Folk Literature. Vol. 2. Bloomington, Indiana University Press, 1956. 6 Vols.

Vance, Garrett Wayne. Personal Interview. April 18, 1996.

Vance, Garrett with Birke Duncan. "The Troll Tale" in The Troll Tale & Other Scary Stories. First edition. Seattle: Northwest Folklore, 2001. 9-26.

Vance, Norman Wm., Jr. Personal interview August 13, 2004.

Virtanen, Leea "That Must Have Been ESP!" An Examination of Psychic Experiences. Trans. John Atkinson & Thomas A. DuBois. Bloomington: Indiana University Press, 1990

Woodward, Walt, ed. "M. Olsen Rites Today. Bainbridge Island Review, November 2, 1945. 1.

_____. "The Story of the 'Standard' Haunts Locals Who Saw Events." Bainbridge Island Review. November 23, 1945. 5.

Chapter 1
The Troll Tale

Bauer, John. Illustrations. John Bauers Sagovarld (John Bauer's World of Stories). Bonniers Juniorforlag AB, 1984 (Bonnier's Junior Publishers, Inc.)

DuBois, Thomas. Lecture at the University of Washington. Seattle. January 31, 1996.

Goldstein, Robert M. Riding with Reindeer: A Bicycle Odyssey Through Finland, Lapland, and Arctic Norway. Seattle: Rivendell Publishing Northwest, 2010.

Rackham, Arthur. Illustrations. The Encyclopedia of Fairies by Katharine Briggs. New York: Pantheon Books, 1976.

Vance, Garrett Wayne. Letters. September 7, 26, 1992, March 24, 1993.

_____. Personal interviews. November 18, 1993, January 23, 25, 31, February 14, 1996.

Woodward, Walt, Editor. "The Story of the 'Standard' Haunts Port Madison Folks Who Saw Events. Bainbridge Island Review. 23 November 1945. 5.

Chapter 2
The Poltergeist Story

Amilien, Virginie. "Troll & Other Supernatural Creatures." Norveg. 1/1996. 39-54.

Briggs, Katharine. The Encyclopedia of Fairies. New York: Pantheon Books, 1976.

De Becker, Gavin. The Gift of Fear: Survival Signals that Protect Us from Violence. New York: Little, Brown, & Co., 1997.

DuBois, Thomas. Lecture at the University of Washington. Seattle. January 31, 1996.

Duncan, Birke. "The Troll Tale" Northwest Folklore. 12.1 (1997) 5-22.

Honko, Lauri. "Memorates & the Study of Folk Belief. Nordic Folklore: Recent Studies. Eds. Reimund Kvideland & Henning Sehmsdorf. Bloomington: Indiana University Press, 1989. 100-109.

Hufford, David. The Terror that Comes in the Night: An Experience Centered Study of Supernatural Assault Traditions. Philadelphia: University of Pennsylvania Press, 1982.

Kvideland, Reimund & Henning Sehmsdorf, Eds. Scandinavian Folk Belief & Legend. Minneapolis: University of Minnesota Press, 1988.

Labov, Wm. & Joshua Waletzky. "Narrative Analysis: Oral Versions of Personal Experience." Essays on the Verbal & Visual Arts. Ed. June Helm. Seattle: University of Washington Press, 1967. 12-44.

Montell, Wm. Lynwood. Ghosts Along the Cumberland. Knoxville: University of Tennessee Press, 1975.

Selberg, Torunn. "Det magiske landskapet" (The Magic Landscape) Tradisjon. Nr. 27. 1/1996. 13-20

Thompson, Stith. Motif-Index of Folk Literature. Vols. 1 & 2. Indiana University Press, 1957.

Vance, Garrett, quoted in "The Troll Tale." Northwest Folklore, 12.1 (1997): 5-22.

_____. Personal interviews. January 23, 25, 31, February 14, 28, APril 4, 9, 25, 1996.

Wyatt, Holly Luidl. Email sent to the author. June 18, 1998.

Chapter 3
Experiences with Fairies
NOTES

1. See, for example "The Fairy Midwife" in Katharine Briggs, A Dictionary of British Folktales–Told Legends, Vol. 1, London: Routledge, 1991) 529. See also "Midwife to the Huldrefolk at Ekeberg" and "Midwife to the Huldrefolk at Nore" in Reidar Christiansen,

Folktales of Norway, Trans. Pat Iversen. University of Chicago Press, 1968.

2.   "The Fairy Dell of Cromarty" is an example of a fairy-haunted mill, and "The Fairies of Langton House" presents a case of fairies taking action against a particular dwelling and family. Briggs, A Dictionary of British Folktales. 215 & 222-224.

3.   "Fairies and the Supernatural of Reachrai." Linda-May Ballard, The Good People: New Fairy Lore Essays. Editor Peter Narvaez (University of Kentucky Press, 1997), 53.

4.   The fairies or huldrefolk (hidden people) of Norwegian folklore also are of human size and appearance. Often these taller beings of British folklore are not recognized as fairies until a display of magical power reveals their nature. As for the huldre, the hidden people's identity may be revealed if someone spots their tale, as in the case of "Outrunning a Hulder", Christiansen.

5.   "Fairylore: Memorates and Legends from Welsh Oral Tradition" Robin Gwyndaf, also from The Good People.

6.   See "The Cormorants from Utrost" for blue clothing and "The Tufte Folk on Sandflesa" where we find "tiny blue-clad people"; both tales from Reidar Christiansen's Folktales of Norway.

7.   Stephen L. Harris. Understanding the Bible. 3rd edition. London: Mayfield Publishing, 1992

8.   Harry T. Burleigh. "Swing Low, Sweet Chariot" in Americana Collection. Ed. Arthur Brandenburg. Chicago: Rubank, Inc., 1942, p. 29. Birke Duncan found the correlation between Ashley's expression and this folk spiritual hymn.

415

Chapter 3
Experiences with Fairies
Works Cited

Bascom, Wm. "Four Functions of Folklore." Journal of American Folklore. 167 (1954): 333-349.

Baughman, Ernest W. Type & Motif-Index of the Folktales of England & North America. Indiana University Folklore Series No. 20. Bloomington: Indiana University Press, 1966.

Bord, Janet. Fairies: Real Encounters with Little People. New York: Dell Publishing, 1997

Briggs, Katharine. A Dictionary of British Folk-Tales. London: Routledge, 1991

_____. The Fairies: In English Tradition & Literature. University of Chicago Press, 1969.

_____. "The Transmission of Folk-Tales in Britain." Folklore, 79 (1968): 81-91

Child, Francis James, ed. The English & Scottish Popular Ballads. Boston: Houghton, Mifflin, & Co., 1885.

Christiansen, Reidar. The Migratory Legends: A Proposed List of Types with a Systematic Catalogue of Norwegian Variants. FF Communications No. 175. Helsinki: Academia Scientarium Fenica, (ASF), 1958.

Degh, Linda. Folktales and Society: Telling in a Hungarian Peasant Community. Trans. Emily M. Schossberger. Indianapolis: Indiana University Press, 1989.

Glassie, Henry, ed. Irish Folk Tales. New York: Pantheon Books, 1985.

Opie, Iona and Moira Tatem, eds. A Dictionary of Superstitions. Oxford University Press, 1989.

416

O Suilleabhain, Sean. The Types of the Irish Folktale. Helsinki: Suomalainen Tiedeakatemia, 1963.

O'Sullivan, Sean. Folktales of Ireland. University of Chicago Press, 1968

Sagan, Carl. The Demon Haunted World. New York: Ballantine Books, 1996.

Sehmsdorf, Henning Kurt. Scandinavian Folk Belief & Legend. Minneapolis: University of Minnesota Press, 1988.

Silver, Carole G. Strange & Secret Peoples: Fairies & Victorian Consciousness. Oxford University Press, 1999.

Tangherlini, Timothy. Interpreting Legend: Danish Storytellers & Their Repertoires. New York: Garland Publishing, 1994.

Thompson, Stith. The Folktale. New York: The Dryden Press, 1951.

_____. Motif-Index of Folk Literature. 1935. 5 Vols. Bloomington: Indiana University Press, 1956.

_____. The Types of Folktale. FF Communications. No. 74. Helsinki: A.S.F., 1927.

Yeats, Wm. Butler. Folktales of the Irish Peasantry. 1888. New York: Gramercy, 1986.

Zipes, Jack, Breaking the Magic Spell: Radical Theories of Folk & Fairy Tales. Austin: University of Texas Press, 1979

_____. Happily Ever After: Fairy Tales, Children, & the Culture Industry. New York: Routledge, 1979.

_____. When Dreams Came True: Classical Fairy Tales & Their Tradition. Routledge, 1999.

Bronner, Simon. "Folk Objects. Folk Groups & Folklore Genres: An Introduction. Ed. Elliott Oring, Logan: Utah State University Press, 1986. 199-233.

Cohen, Hennig. "Going to See the Widow." Journal of American Folklore. 64/252 (1951): 223

Costello, Hon. Leonard. Order Committing the Defendant to Western State Hospital. Kitsap County Superior Court, Port Orchard, Washington. Case #93-1-00-470-1. May 28, 1993.

Cronin, Mary Elizabeth. "Storyteller Jackie Torrence's Hisses & Howls Will Grab You." Seattle Times. May 21, 1998. E 1-2.

De Becker, Gavin. The Gift of Fear. New York: Little, Brown, & Co. 1997.

Douglas, John. Lecture presented at the University Bookstore, Seattle, 1999.

Douglas, John E. & Mark Olshaker. Obsession. New York: Simon & Schuster, 1998

_____. The Anatomy of Motive. Simon & Schuster, 1999.

DuBois, Thomas. Lecture at the University of Washington. Seattle, January 31, 1996.

Duncan, Birke. "The Troll Tale." Northwest Folklore 12.1 (1997): 5-22.

Hall, Gary. "The Big Tunnel." Indiana Folklore: A Reader. Ed. Linda Degh. Indiana University Press, 1980. 225-257.

Hart, R.M. Letter to Hon. Leonard Costello. Dept. of Social & Health Services Mental Health Evaluation. Kitsap County Superior Court. Case #93-1-00-470-1. June 23, 1993.

Holbrook, Hal. Adaptation. Mark Twain Tonight! 1959.

Hutchison, Kristan. "They Thought it was a Gag." Bainbridge Review. June 2, 1993. A4.

Knowles, John. A Separate Peace. Scribner, 1959

Korkiakangas, Pirjo. "Childhood Memories & Conceptualisation of Childhood. Ethnologia Scandinavica. 24 (1994): 60-69.

Lindow, John. "Supernatural Others & Ethnic Others." Scandinavian Studies. 67.1 (1994): 8-31.

McAllister, Robert Charles. Personal interviews. April 25, May 9, 1997. October 28, 1998; June 23, July 29, 1999.

Nash, Jay Robert. "Reagan, Ronald Wilson." The Encyclopedia of World Crime. Vol. 3. Wilmette, Illinois: Crime Books Inc., 1990. 2549-2550.

Palmer, Verina "Student Claims God Sent Him on Mission." Bainbridge Review. June 2, 1993 A5.

_____. "Student Found Mentally Competent." Bainbridge Review. July 27, 1993. A3.

Prout, David and Julia Thomas. Victim Impact Statements. Kitsap County Superior Court. Case #93-1-00-470-1. July 14, 1993.

Ressler, Robert and Tom Schachtman. I Have Lived in the Monster. New York: St. Martin's Press, 1997.

Slater, Eric. "Manhunt Intensifies." Seattle Times. June 23, 1999. A3.

Tangherlini, Timothy. "From Trolls to Turks: Continuity & Change in Danish Legend Tradition." Scandinavian Studies. 67.1 (1994) 32-62.

Wojcik, Daniel. The End of the World as We Know It: Faith, Fatalism, & Apocalypse in America. New York University Press, 1997.

Chapter 5
Three Anti-Memorats

Archives. Bainbridge Island Historical Museum. Bainbridge Island, Washington.

Briggs, Katharine. A Dictionary of British Folk-Tales in the English Language. Part A. Folk Narratives. Vol. 1. London: Routledge & Kagan Paul 1970.

Cheadle, Ralph. Lecture at Bainbridge High School, Bainbridge Island, Washington, Oct. 1983.

_____. Personal interview. August 31, 1999.

DuBois, Thomas. Lecture at the University of Washington. January 31, 1996.

Duncan Birke & Robert McAllister. "The River Boys: An Oral Short Story." Northwest Folklore. 13.7 (1999): 27-46

Exorcist, The. Dir. Wm. Friedkin. Warner Bros. 1973.

Hawthorne, Nathaniel. The Scarlet Letter. 1850. New York: Dodd, Mead, & Co., 1948.

Honko, Lauri. "Memorates & the Study of Folk Belief." Nordic Folklore. Indiana University Press, 1989. 100-109.

Irving, Washington. "The Legend of Sleepy Hollow." in The Sketch Book. 1819. The MacMillan Co., 1913. 326-360.

Kvideland, Reimund & H.K. Sehmsdorf. Scandinavian Folk Belief & Legend. University of Minnesota Press, 1988.

Lovecraft, H.P. "The Call of Cthulhu." The Best of H.P. Lovecraft. New York: Ballantine Books, 1963. 75-99.

Seymour, St. John & Harry Neligan. True Irish Ghost Stories. 1914. New York: Galahad Books, 1992.

Simon, Danny. Lectures at the University of Washington. Seattle. March 6-8, 1992.

Strong, Sanford. Strong on Defense: Survival Rules to Protect You & Your Family from Crime. Simon & Schuster 1996.

Thompson, Stith. Motif-Index of Folk Literature. Vols. 3, 5. Indiana University Press, 1957.

Tongue, Ruth, collector. "Crooker" in A Dictionary of British Folk-Tales in the English Language London: Routledge &: Kagan Paul, 1970. 195-197.

Vance, Garrett. Personal interview. May 8, 1997.

Wizard of Oz, The. Dir. Victor Fleming. MGM. 1939.

Chapter 6
Shadows of Tradition
NOTES

1. "Seven out of Ten American Families Will Be Giving Out Treats This Halloween." The Gallup Poll Organization, October 29, 1999, http://www.gallup.com/poll/releases/pr991039.asp

2. Katharine Briggs, The Fairies: In English Tradition & Literature (Chicago: University of Chicago Press, 1969, 19 & 51, et al.

3. An example of the giant being in "The Great Giant of Henllys." Katharine Briggs. A Dictionary of British Folk-Tales–Folk Legends, Vol. 1., (London, Routledge, 1991) 487.

4. An example is "Madame Gould: II" in: Briggs, A Dictionary. 529

5. Timothy Tangherlini in Interpreting Legend offers evidence for "the interface between" the "man-made" and the "natural" in his exploration of

legends and memorates where "human control" is represented by the man-made features, and implicitly, though Tangherlini does not fully articulate the view, the natural connotes a coded threat to civilization. Timothy Tangherlini Interpreting Legend–Danish Storytellers and Their Repertoires (New York: Garland Publishing, Inc., 1994) 131-132.

6. Briggs, The Fairies, 82-83.

7. Motifs include F456.1.1.2 "Knockers are ghosts of giants who formerly lived in the area." F 456.1.1.3 "Knockers are spirits of dead miners." Ernest Baughman, Type and Motif-Index of the Folktales of England and North America. Indiana University Folklore Series No. 20. (Bloomington: Indiana University Press, 1966) 226.

8. Accounts of only one person seeing a ghost are most common but Stith Thompson has a motif for cases like Birke and Andrews where verification occurs E421.5 "Ghost seen by two or more persons; they corroborate the appearance."

9. The appearance of the revenant as an old man is an international motif (E 424.2.1 "Revenant as old man").

10. A Sallet. Les esprits malfaisants dans les affections epidemiques au Bin Thuan" Bulletin des amis du vieux Hue 13.1 (Jan.-March 1926), 81-88.

11. Dia Cha, and Norma J. Livo, Folk Stories of the Hmong–Peoples of Laos, Thailand, and Vietnam (Englewood: Libraries Unlimited, Inc., 1991) 3.

12. Gabriell, Gertrand, The Jungle People–Men, beast, and legends of the Moi country (London: Robert Hale Ltd, 1959) 27.

13-14. Dia Cha, & Norma Livo, Folk stories of the Hmong, 3

15. Le Tinh Thong, Popular Stories from Vietnam, Vol 2., (San Diego State University– Institute for Cultural Pluralism, 1976), 41-49.

16. "The Rope Ghost" is in Le Tinh Thong Popular 39. "Histoire du demon de Xuong Giang" is found in: Du, Nguyen, sixteenth century Vaste Recueil de Legendes Merveilleuses, (Paris: Gallimard, c 1962), 155-162. The reference to the king of hell occurs: 159-162.

17. The quotation is from the notes accompanying the story. 100.

18. One example of the appearance of the wraith is in "The Dance of Death" where a young man seems to appear to dance, yet he has at that very moment died elsewhere. Briggs, A Dictionary, 433.

19. A good example of the wraith, or Fetch as it is called in Ireland and England, is in "The Doctor's Fetch" where a man not only sees his fetch, but his wife sees it, too; and these visions occur while the man seems to be sleeping. Briggs, A Dictionary 433.

20. Briggs, A Dictionary, Vol 2 594-595.

21. Dr. Thomas DuBois, who knows both German and Norwegian, contributed to this analysis by translating the following sources: Lily Weisne-Aall, "En studie om vardoeger [Eine Studie uber den Folgegeist] [A Study of the Following Spirit] Norveg 12 (1965), 73-112. Kurt Ranke, "Doppelganger" Enzyklopadie des Marchens, Band 3 (Berlin: Walter De Gruyter, 1981), 766-771. The quotation is from Dr. DuBois's synopsis of "En studie om vardoeger."

22.   Reference to the doubles of all four authors appear in "Kurt Ranke "Doppelganger"", Encyclopedia, 767. Accounts of doubles of Goethe and Maupassant are given in Claudie Dembriski, et al, eds, Encyclopedia of Occultism & Parapsychology, 4 vols. (Detroit: Gale Research Co, 1978), 257-258. The claim for Shelley is mentioned in the website for Encyclopedia Mythica: http://pantheon.org/mythica/articles/d/doppelganger.html

23.   The Encyclopedia of Occultism & Parapsychology relates an account of St. Anthony of Padua who in 1226 sent his spirit forth to "the other end of town" to preach (254). Also Alphonse de Liguori, who in September 17, 1774 though he was imprisoned elsewhere supposedly was able to minister "at the death bed of Pope Clement XIV"(254).

24.   LeeaVirtanen includes several examples in her section on "Hallucinations" in "That Must Have Been ESP!"

25.   Katharine Briggs, An Encyclopedia of Fairies (New York: Pantheon Books, 1976), 80.

26.   Please email any information on the doppelganger, Vietnamese demonology, etc. to jasonmarcharris@ gmail.com

27.   W.A.Clouston Popular Tales and Fictions–Their Migrations & Transformations 2 Vols., 13-14.

28.   Some other motifs involving assuming the likeness of another include D40 "Transformation to likeness of another person." F234.2 "Fairy in form of a person." K1952.0.0 Brahman taking shape of a prince. D402.1 "Transformation to resemble man's mistress so as to be able to kill him." D49.2 "Spirit takes any form." The account of both

Amphitryon and Solomon and Asmodeus is generally alluded to in the following work: Kurt Ranke, Enzyklopedia 768. Regarding Amphitryon, I consulted Sir Paul Harvey, The Oxford Companion to Classical Literature (Oxford University Press, 1984), 25. There may well be undocumented tale-type here in the fact that in both the Mongolian tale and the Amphitryon fable the deception occurs to a soldier returning from war. The French film, The Return of Martin Guerre and its American remake Sommersby have a similar subject.

29.   The specific Talmudic details—regarding the wives and Bathsheba are found in: Raphael Patai,Gates to the Old City–A Book of Jewish Legends (New York: Avon Books, 1980) 185-188. Asmodeus's transformation is not perfect; his feet betray him–Near Eastern myths since the Sumerians attribute bird-like talons to demons. In Western European traditions, there is a similar belief: the devil has hooves. Bathsheba grew suspicious as well at the request for copulation; see Angelo Rappoport, Myth & Legend of Ancient Israel, Vol.3 (New York: KTAV Publishing House, 1966), 138-139.

30.   Motifs of the second sight include: D1825.1 "Second Sight: Power to see future happenings." D1825.3 "Magic power to see invisible creatures." D1825.3.3 "Magic sight: ability to see the soul (astral body). D1825.3.3.1 "Magic power to see souls after death." D1825.3.4 "Ability to see heavenly beings."

31.   Lily Weiser-Aall, "En studie om vardoeger" [A Study of the Following Spirit] Norveg 12 (1965), 73-112.

32. Motifs include: J157 "Wisdom (knowledge) from a dream. E361.0.1 "Dead appears in dream... E720.1 "Souls of human beings seen in dream." D1812.3.3 "Future revealed in dream."

33. In "Laying Wild Harris's Ghost," a group of black spirits threaten the clergymen who are attempting to exorcise a man's ghost. Briggs, A Dictionary,Vol.1 518-522.

34. In "The Knight of Malta" there is an example of a floating ghost. Briggs, A Dictionary Vol. 1, 508-509.

35. Spirits in the form of shadows are not unprecedented, however. Chris's description of the shadowy figure in his home sounds very much like a fairy, and Thompson includes motifs associating shadows with both fairies & ghosts: E421.4 "Ghosts as shadow." F235.7 "Fairies seen as dark shadow." Indeed, there is not always a clear distinction between fairies and spirits of the dead.

36. Sith Thompson discusses the "epic laws"of Olrik; he notes that Olrik was aware that the threefold structure sometimes was fourfold because of "religious symbolism" in a particular culture. However, there does not seem to be any religious symbolism involved in Samuel Barton's structure. Stith Thompson, The Folktale (New York: Dryden Press, 1951) 456.

37. This information is from a conversation that arose during a meeting with Dr. Adams on April 30, 1999.

38. Stith Thompson, The Types of the Folk-Tale–A Classification & Biography: Anti Aarne's Verzeidnis der Marchentypen FF communications No 74 (Helsinki, ASF, 1927).

39.	Daniel Levy, "The Last Taboo" Time June 28, 1999, 77.

Shadows of Tradition
Works Cited

Baughman, Ernest. Type & Motif-Index of the Folktales of England & North America. Indiana University Press. Folklore Series. No. 20., 1966.

Bertrand, Gabrielle.The Jungle People:Men, Beasts, & Legends of the Moi Country. Trans. Eleanor Brockett. London: Robert Hale. Ltd. 1959.

Briggs, Katharine. A Dictionary of Folk-Tales. London: Routledge, 1991.

_____. An Encyclopedia of Fairies. New York: Pantheon Books, 1976.

_____. The Fairies. University of Chicago Press, 1969.

Cha, Dia & Norma Livo. Folk Stories of the Hmong: Peoples of Laos, Thailand, & Vietnam. Englewood: Libraries Unlimited, Inc. 1991.

Child, Francis, ed. The English & Scottish Popular Ballads. Boston: Houghton, Mifflin, & Co., 1885.

Christiansen, Reider. The Migratory Legends: A Proposed List of Types. FF Communications No. 175. Helsinki: ASF, 1958.

Clouston, W.A. Popular Tales & Fictions. 2 Vols. Edinburgh: Wm. Blackwood & Sons, 1968.

Dembinski, Claudia, ed., Encyclopedia of Occultism & Parapsychology. 4 Vols. Detroit: Gale Research Co, 1978.

Harvey, Sir Paul. The Oxford Companion to Classical Literature. Oxford University Press, 1984.

Jones, Alison. Larousse Dictionary of World Folklore. Edinburgh: Larousse plc, 1995.

Lang, Andrew.The Book of Dreams & Ghosts.1897.New York: Causeway Books, 1974.

Laveissiere, Maite. Contes Du Viet-Nam. Coubrong: Pierru, 1968.

Levy, Daniel S. "The Last Taboo." Time. June 28, 1999.

Narvaez, Peter, ed. The Good People. University of Kentucky Press, 1997.

Nguyen, Dong Chi. Trans. L'Hymenee dans le Reve. Paris: Sudestasie, 1987.

Nguyen, Du. 16th century. Vaste Recueil de Legendes Merveilleuses. Paris: Gallimard, 1962.

Opie, Iona & Moira Tatem, Eds. A Dictionary of Superstitions. Oxford University Press, 1989.

Patai, Raphael. Gates to the Old City: A Book of Jewish Legends. Oxford University Press, 1989

Ranke, Kurt, ed. Enzyklopadie des Marchens. New York: Walter De Gruyter, 1981.

Rappoport, Angelo. Myth & Legend of Ancient Israel. 3 Vols. New York: KTAV Publishing House, 1966.

Ross, Anne. The Folklore of the Scottish Highlands. New York: Barnes & Noble Books, 1976.

Salles,A."Les esprits malfaisants dans les affections epidemiques au binh Thuan." Bulletin des amis du vieux Hue. 13.1 (January to March 1926).

Schultz, George F., Trans. Vietnamese Legends. Vermont: Chas. E. Tuttle Co., 1965.

Sehmsdorf, Henning. Scandinavian Folk Belief & Legend. University of Minnesota Press, 1988.

Tangherlini, Timothy. Interpreting Legend. New York: Garland Publishing, 1994.

Thompson, Stith. The Folktale. New York: The Dryden Press, 1951.

_____. Motif-Index of Folk Literature. 1935. 5 Vols. Indiana University Press, 1956.

_____. The Types of Folktale. FF Communications. No. 74. Helsinki: ASF, 1927.

Thong, Le Tinh. Popular Stories from Vietnam. Vol 2. San Diego State University, 1976.

Virtanen Leea. "That Must Have Been Esp!" Indiana University Press, 1990.

Webber, Andrew J. The Doppelganger: Double Visions in German Literature. Oxford: Clarendon Press, 1996.

Weiser-Aal, Lily. "En studie om vardoger [Eine Studie uber den Folgegeist.] Norveg. 12 (1965): 73-112

Wildhaber, Robert, ed. International Folklore and Folklife Bibliography. Bonn, Germany. Rudolf Habelt Verlag, 1969.

Zucchelli, P. Florent. Contes populaires du Viet-nam d'autrefois. N.p.: Cocconier, 1968

About the Authors

Jason Marc Harris, Ph.D., teaches creative writing, folklore, and literature, plus he serves as the Creative Writing Coordinator at Texas A&M University in College Station, TX. He is the author of *Master of Rods & Strings* (Vernacular Books, 2021) and *Folklore & the Fantastic in Nineteenth Century British Fiction* (Routledge, 2008). He has also written many short stories and scholarly folklore articles.

Birke R. Duncan, M.A. is a magician, puppeteer, and filmmaker. He and Jason Harris collaborated on *The Troll Tale & Other Scary Stories* (Northwest Folklore, 2001) and *Laugh without Guilt: A Clean Joke Book* (Northwest Folklore, 2007). They also wrote the short comedy film *The Adventures of Monty Moudlyn*.

Several short films and radio plays are now available on the Birke Duncan YouTube Channel, plus two featurettes on the Kevin Veatch YouTube Channel. *A Janitor's Territory* and *Runaway Imagination* rely upon folklore.

Mr. Duncan is married to author and artist Sara Mossman Duncan.

Authors' Note to the Reader

Thank you.

Made in the USA
Monee, IL
15 July 2022

99729426R00243